A Story to Live By

Kathy Galloway is a theologian and poet. She is a member of the Iona Community and editor of its magazine, *Coracle*. She lives in Glasgow, works ecumenically with local churches and groups encouraging theology and community development, and travels widely as a consultant and speaker. Her poems and liturgical writings have been widely anthologized.

OTHER TITLES BY KATHY GALLOWAY

Imagining the Gospels (Triangle, new edition 1994)
Love Burning Deep (SPCK 1993)
Struggles to Love (SPCK 1994)
Getting Personal (SPCK 1995)
Pushing the Boat Out (edited) (Wild Goose Publications 1995)
Talking to the Bones (SPCK 1996)
The Pattern of Our Days (edited) (Wild Goose Publications 1996)
Dreaming of Eden: Reflections on Christianity and Sexuality
    (Wild Goose Publications 1997)
Starting Where We Are: Liberation Theology in Practice
    (Wild Goose Publications 1998)

A Story to Live By

Kathy Galloway

First published in Great Britain in 1999
Society for Promoting Christian Knowledge
Holy Trinity Church
Marylebone Road
London NW1 4DU

British Library Cataloguing-in-Publication Data
A catalogue record for this book is available from the British Library

ISBN 0-281-05164-X

Typeset by David Gregson Associates, Beccles, Suffolk
Printed in Great Britain by The Cromwell Press, Trowbridge, Wiltshire

Contents

To the Iona Community
with love and gratitude

I wish to thank a number of people and organizations without whose help this book would not have been written. The work of the Steering Committee of Scottish Churches Action for World Development/Common Weal, 1990–96 was the originator of the Development for Life programme, and the contributions of Alistair Hulbert, Elizabeth South, Alistair McIntosh, Helen Steven, Meredyth Somerville, Yvonne Burgess, Kate Houston and Yvonne Morland have been invaluable and inspirational. Thanks go also to the Joseph Rowntree Charitable Trust and to the Iona Community, who funded the work for a year.

The editorial staff of SPCK have been, as always, helpful and patient. I thank them too: Joanna Moriarty, Kathryn Wolfendale, Deborah Adams and Jennifer Wild. Their care for the book has been encouraging.

I am always impressed by those authors who thank the providers of rural retreats and academic sanctuaries where they can write in quiet. My life, alas, is not like that, so instead I thank David, Duncan and Helen for taking the rubbish out, cleaning the bathroom, and making me endless cups of coffee. I would not be without their constant interruptions, which come in equal measure to their constant enthusiasm.

Most of all, I wish to thank those people who shared their stories with me and with one another.

This book is dedicated to the Iona Community, whose theologians, poets and storytellers have informed my understanding, and whose story to live by is also mine.

Introduction:
Development for Life

In 1992, I was funded by the Joseph Rowntree Charitable Trust, Scottish Churches Action for World Development (now CommonWeal) and the Iona Community to create, pilot and use a series of learning workshop modules on culture and development. The purpose of these was to develop a method whereby ordinary people could reflect on their own experience, their own culture, history and geography, and on how these interact with the changing world around them. Simply put, it was an attempt to help people look at the stories they live by, and at all the factors that shape these stories.

This work had its origins in the concerns of Scottish Churches Action for World Development (SCAWD). Set up to raise awareness in Scotland about global issues of poverty and development, we were struggling in our work with two particular difficulties. One was the tendency for many in the West to see poverty in the countries of the South as being the result of Southern fecklessness, ignorance, overpopulation, war – in effect, as 'their fault', and to feel that 'charity begins at home', without taking on board the complex causes of poverty, and the role of the West through colonialism and exploitation in helping to impoverish the so-called 'third world'. In an attempt to move from a charitable approach to aid to a justice-based approach, we wanted to make the links between poverty in Britain and poverty in the world's poorest countries more visible.

The second difficulty lay in addressing the recognized and well-documented failures of the predominant development models since the Second World War. Because so many development initiatives and projects were too exclusively based on Western ideas of progress, economics, social life and values, technology and so on,

1

many of them have actually damaged the communities they sought to support, have uprooted and weakened them, and have alienated them from their own cultural and spiritual roots and resources.

Linked to this is many people's sense of powerlessness at being the object of external (and often alien) notions of progress, rather than being able to be the subjects of their own self-development. Being told 'This is what will make you happy', and having your own knowledge of what will make you happy ignored, is a most disempowering experience. People's experience was unheard, their knowledge and wisdom derided, and their spiritual and cultural values denied. They were being excluded, not just from setting the goals of their development, but from shaping its means.

And this sense of powerlessness is also found in the West, especially among those whom society often designates as 'losers' or 'the underclass'. It was with this concern that SCAWD was working on finding new ways of enabling people to look at broad issues of human development that took as their starting point people's own stories and experience (especially those of people who do not often find these valued or respected), and from that starting point to widen out to look at other experiences, other stories in a way that respected differences while seeking for the common ground.

These workshops were given the title, 'Development for Life'. They sought to enable people to 'put themselves in the picture'. They asked:

- what is my story?
- what has helped to shape my story?
- how does my story relate to the stories of others?

Each workshop was based on one of the basic life questions that people in all kinds of societies ask themselves: Why am I here? Where do I belong? Who am I? What really matters? How do I care? How do we live together though we are different?

Since then, and well past the time of the original finding, I have travelled the length and breadth of Scotland and England, with occasional trips into Ireland and Wales, giving these workshops; to church and community groups, women's groups, schools, colleges and other interested groups and organizations, with a particular emphasis on working with people living in poverty. I have done dozens of workshops with hundreds of people. I have heard many moving stories, some of them tragic, some full of hope, almost all remarkable for their courage. And of course, it has made me reflect deeply on my own personal and political story. I have thought about the history and geography and culture and experience and faith which have made me the person I am.

This book is the product of that work. It is not the writing-up of research, or an academic treatise. It is more an extended reflection on the story I live by, the common ground it shares with the stories of others, and on our differences. And as someone whose story has been deeply shaped by Christianity, there is a big question for me underlying my reflection – is Christian faith still a story to live by on the cusp of a new millennium? I hold some convictions dear which are held by many who are not Christian, who are of other faiths, are humanist, are atheist. Does being a Christian make a difference for me in holding to these convictions?

And it is my hope that this book might encourage people to think about their own stories, to value the wealth of experience that all of them contain, and to appreciate anew the delight of sharing the stories of others.

> In any street an epic, any room
> Strange stories never told, testaments dumb.
> The richness overwhelms. A chance remark
> Can touch new land, unload another ark.
> Transactions of small change will sometimes yield
> Coins of a minting you have never held.
> Break any casual stone and find strange veins,
> The colours blind. The anecdotes will range
> Through wild geographies of spirit, form.
> Plain men with unknown flowers in their arms.
> In each face, new horizons, any day
> An archeology more rich than Troy.
> (William McIlvanney)

A Story to Live By

Why, who makes much of a miracle?
As to me I know of nothing else but miracles,
Whether I walk the streets of Manhattan,
Or dart my sight over the roofs of houses toward the sky,
Or wade with naked feet along the beach just in the edge of the
    water,
Or stand under trees in the woods,
Or talk by day with any one I love, or sleep in the bed at night with
    any one I love,
Or sit at table at dinner with the rest,
Or look at strangers opposite me riding in the car,
Or watch honey-bees busy around the hive of a summer forenoon,
Or animals feeding in the fields,
Or birds, or the wonderfulness of insects in the air,
Or the wonderfulness of the sundown, or of stars shining so quiet
    and bright,
Or the exquisite delicate thin curve of the new moon in spring;
These with the rest, one and all, are to me miracles,
The whole referring, yet each distinct and in its place.
To me every hour of the light and dark is a miracle,
Every cubic inch of space is a miracle,
Every square yard of the surface of the earth is spread with the same,
Every foot of the interior swarms with the same.

To me the sea is a continual miracle,
The fishes that swim – the rocks – the motion of the waves – the ships
    with men in them,
What stranger miracles are there?

(Walt Whitman, 'Miracles', 1950)

I first read this poem by Walt Whitman when I was about fifteen. I loved it then, and I love it still. It struck me with all the force of recognition, that experience of seeing something expressed, and knowing instantly a great 'yes'. Yes, this is what I believe, yes, this is how it is for me.

I think on reflection, I was saying yes to three distinct yet referring principles. The first was a conviction of the goodness of the whole creation, not goodness in a moral sense, but ontologically, the goodness of being. All is good, not by virtue of its value to others, or by its resourcefulness or its efficiency, but simply in the fact of its being. It is a principle of intrinsic worth, the same principle that is celebrated in the first chapter of the book of Genesis ('and it was very good' (1.31)), that is displayed in the foundational creation stories of so many cultures and faiths.

And this particular expression of intrinsic worth spoke to me as someone brought up in and loving the city. This was not just a celebration of nature, but of the integrity of nature and culture. Here was someone who did not see any contradiction in loving a city skyline as much as the new moon, the flow of conversation as much as the hum of bees, who felt no necessity to place them in competition, opposition, or order of merit. All were good.

The second principle I was saying yes to was the conviction not only of the intrinsic worth of the creation, but of its interconnectedness. Part of its goodness lay not only in its existence but in its relatedness – or rather, that existence could not be separated from that relatedness. In Whitman's poem, the whole universe exists in a delicate yet complex web of relationship, in which even the language by which we recognize and name relatedness is itself a component. We, all of us, exist in relationship with the very air we breathe, we are part of it, without it we have no existence, just as we have no existence without the act of conception which brought us into being, which in its turn was contingent on billions of acts of conception of one kind or another.

At the very end of the twentieth century, we are much more aware of our interdependency with all other life forms – physicists, biologists, ecologists and scientists of every discipline have made sure that we can no longer plead ignorance – but Whitman, writing before Einstein, in a scientific world that was still static and dualistic, spoke out of the intuitive wisdom of the artist and lover – which is, of course, the same wisdom that very small children have just as a result of using their senses, before it is socialized out of them. I remember my daughter, aged about two years, going to bed with a nightly ritual that went something like 'goodnight Mummy, goodnight Daddy, goodnight boys, goodnight teddy, goodnight sky, goodnight sea, goodnight sheep, goodnight birds, goodnight table, goodnight door' – and on and on until my stamina ran out at the prospect of naming the universe.

This interconnectedness, this integrity of creation, has been recognized always by poets and prophets and by religion that takes care, that reveres and sees the sacred. It is what Jesus was expressing in John's Gospel: ' "I am the vine and you are the branches" (15.5). "A branch cannot bear fruit by itself; it can do so only if it remains in the vine" ' (15.4). Or, more lately, in these words of prayer by George MacLeod, the founder of the Iona Community:

> In You, all things consist and hang together:
> The very atom is light energy,
> The grass is vibrant,
> The rocks pulsate.
> All is in flux; turn but a stone and an angel moves.
>
> (*The Whole Earth Shall Cry Glory*, 1985)

And the third principle I was saying yes to in Whitman's poem as a description of truth for me was the conviction that nothing is more miraculous, more wonderful, more worthy of reverence, than the ordinary. Streets and trees, buses and birds, eating dinner and sleeping with someone loved – all such ordinary, accessible, habitual things, and yet all extraordinary. I knew that this articulated for me an incredible frustration that people should be so obsessed with searching for something else, while ignoring, devaluing and desecrating what they had right under their noses. This frustration, I confess, was considerably exacerbated by years in an academic study of theology, listening to interminable arguments (mostly among the students, it should be said) about the exact nature of the miracles of Jesus. It was not so much a disagreement with the answers, as an unhappy feeling that the questions entirely missed the point. What lack of imagination, insight, vision, blinded people to seeing simply what was there? Again, it was the poets who expressed it for me best – George MacLeod, praying:

> In all created things Thou art there.
> In every friend we have
> the sunshine of Thy presence is shown forth.

In every enemy that seems to cross our path,
Thou art there within the cloud
to challenge us to love.
Show to us the glory in the grey.

('The Glory in the Grey', 1985)

Or the American writer, Alice Walker:

We alone can devalue gold
by not caring
if it falls or rises
in the market place.
Wherever there is gold
there is a chain, you know,
and if your chain
is gold
so much the worse
for you.

Feathers, shells
and sea-shaped stones
are all as rare.
This could be our revolution:
To love what is plentiful
as much as
what's scarce.

('We Alone', 1984)

Looking back over my life, I see that it has been guided and shaped by these three distinct yet referring principles: the conviction of intrinsic worth; the conviction of the relatedness of all things; the conviction of the miraculousness of the ordinary, the glory in the grey. These convictions I know I share with people in every part of the world, of every background, race and religion, in every culture and condition. I am not alone in these convictions. They are a profound motivation, a spirituality, for many who are lovers of life. For me, they are a story to live by.

A different way of seeing

I live in a Western country (Scotland), in an era which is democratic, pluralist, multicultural, and in which people follow many different faiths and none. Christianity, which is the faith in which I was brought up, as an institution, has been throughout its history, for the most part, patriarchal (ruled by and in the interests of men),

7

authoritarian, and has sought to impose its own dominant Western culture on the places (including those within Britain) where it has evangelized. The tensions between these two different ways of seeing the world are self-evident. Some parts of the church try to make the world fit into the old pattern. Some parts divide their seeing, embracing the newer pattern in their secular, 'weekday' lives, while maintaining the old in their religious, 'Sunday' lives. Some parts struggle to find a new way of being the church consistent with the values they hold dear in the world. So there are Christians clinging for dear life to the old world order which existed at a time when it was more or less identical to the church's. There are Christians in transition. And there are Christians who have paid, and continue to pay a price for being in the front line, not only of the church's transition, but of the world's. In all this, there is a lot of confusion. What should be our story to live by?

The hard-won struggle of the individual to be the subject of his or her own life (which is by no means won for everyone) has contributed to, and flowed from such changes this century as the universal franchise, equal opportunities legislation with regard to ethnicity and gender, changes in family law, the opening up of continuing education to a much greater part of the population, and the explosion in information technology. One of the consequences of this is an altered relationship to authority of all kinds. People ask questions, and will not be satisfied with platitudes or clichés or dogma in answer. Institutions of every kind come under close scrutiny. 'Because I say so' is no longer an adequate response in any context.

And despite a vast amount of information, despite ever-increasing scientific knowledge, despite all the confusion and tensions – or perhaps because of all these things – people still do ask questions. We still struggle to find meaning in our lives, or even the meaning of our lives. Faced with a smorgasbord of choices, sometimes we stick to what we have always known, even if that means closing our minds and stunting our lives. Sometimes we make choices which are self-destructive, or which cause huge 'collateral damage'. And sometimes we are paralysed by the demands of choice.

> for the question is always
> how
> out of all the chances and changes
> to select

the features of real significance
   so as to make
of the welter
  a world that will last
and how to order
   the signs and the symbols
so they will continue
  to form new patterns
developing into
new harmonic wholes
  so to keep life alive
in complexity
  and complicity
   with all of being –
there is only poetry

(Kenneth White, 'Extract I' from 'A Walk along the Shore', 1974)

Writing in the *Guardian* under the headline, 'God is not dead, he was only voted out', the cultural commentator Mark Lawson reflected on the findings of a recent MORI poll that only 43 per cent of Britons now believe in God, and drew a parallel between political and religious trends. He wrote: 'The 24% disparity in the poll ratings for God and for religion (67% of those polled regarded themselves as religious) suggests that organised worship has simply given way to displacement faith, just as organised democracy has given way to displacement politics' (June 1997).

Perhaps those polled, like so many others, are also struggling with the question so pertinently raised by Kenneth White's poem, of how, out of all the chances and changes with which life at the end of the twentieth century is beset, to select the features of real significance and how to order the signs and the symbols into new patterns, paradigms and wholes. And just as many people have lost faith in party politics and politicians, and have turned to single-issue campaigning or other alternative political forms, so, the report suggests, people are turning from mainstream Christian churches into a whole range of alternative cults, spiritualities and therapies.

The theological task

In his poem, Kenneth White refines the question 'how' into two imperatives. 'How to select' is a spiritual question, 'how to order' is a political one.

'How to select the features of real significance': To select is a grown-up thing to do. When we are small children, the world is full of desirable things, and we want to have them all, and think we can. As we grow up, we learn, sooner or later, that we must choose, decide, and that that is hard and often painful. It means making priorities, evaluating, weighing up alternatives. And yet it is a necessary part of maturity. Not to decide is also to decide.

'How to order the signs and the symbols': It is in this ordering task that we assume author-ity, the writing of the script of the world, or our part of it at least. And because the script always involves other people, even if not as the main actors, it is a political task, it involves the use of power. This century has seen shocking examples of what can happen when those who take it upon themselves to order the signs and symbols for great numbers of people claim absolute authority of the kind that used to be attributed only to God, or the gods. The line that divides ordering from controlling and then from oppressing is very thin. But most of us, in as simple a thing as casting a vote in an election, take upon ourselves some measure of participation in ordering the signs and symbols.

And for people of religious conviction, inclination or yearning, the question of how to select and how to order is a theological one. It involves words about God, or the Word of God, and the different ways in which we understand, or do not understand, these.

Whether we define ourselves as religious or not, selecting the features of real significance and ordering the signs and symbols is both a tall order and an ongoing human quest. Historically, people have found meaning in their lives, their story to live by, in a number of ways.

They have found it in their relationship to the land and the sea, and have understood these as the ground of their being, that which gave their lives purpose and value. Or they have found it in their work, which was not always defined as waged labour (though clearly people in, for example, mining or shipbuilding found their meaning in their jobs). Or they found it in their participation in a community, a tribe, a clan, a city, that was stable, sometimes for centuries, had clear boundaries about who belonged, and in which many rituals allowed for the artful transfer of knowledge about how to live from one generation to another. And they found it in their religion, ideology or symbolic structure, in which they could live lives transfigured by ceremony and conviction.

All of these brought both gifts and wounds, a light but also a shadow: the back-breaking, relentless grind, and sometimes the absolute destitution or the cruel danger experienced by those who lived from land and sea; the exploitation, grim conditions, destruction of health and sheer lack of recognition of much work; the brutal exclusion and scapegoating of those who stepped outside the community norms; the use of religion and ideology as a means of domination and control.

Whatever our own feelings about the relative merits of gift and wound in these ways of being, the fact remains that all of them have been subjected to a breaking process – a shaking of the foundations – which has also shaken people loose from them as a source of meaning. The timescale may have been different in different countries and parts of the world, but the process of deconstruction of what had been considered eternal, unshakeable, has been the same.

When people lose *meaning*, a story to live by, they also lose other important things. They lose a sense of *belonging*, a place or people or context where they are at home; and their sense of *identity*, of knowing who they are. Of course, these things are not static, they are dynamic, always in the process of coming into being, only becoming self-conscious as we attempt to name them.

Who are we, trapped in our ways
   Of dying towards the fact
of only once having been, together
or separate in our own being
   But never wholly separate, only a part
of the time we live in, and with others occupy

(Tom Leonard, 'Proem', 1995)

But when people become disconnected from things like land, work, community and symbolic system, the yearning for meaning, belonging, identity, remains. We suffer their loss as a bereftness, seek to recreate them elsewhere if we can; or suppress the grief and enter a void. Perhaps our obsession with busyness and growth and filling every physical and aural space is symptomatic of a present without depth.

In that loss, or that void, much has been thrown on to other things to fill the gap, to restore meaning and belonging and identity.

- The nuclear family has had a burden of expectation thrown on to it, of meeting all the needs and aspirations of its members, that has simply proved too great to carry. It is cracking under the strain.
- The nation state, a political construct which has had varying degrees

of success, is always at risk of being understood as a destructive cultural or ethnic nationalism.

- The superstate, as the former Soviet Union or the European Community may be described, is usually too big, too remote, to meet the hunger to have our personhood affirmed. It is hard for most people to feel passionate about Europe.

- The marketplace constantly exhorts us, and we try, to find meaning, belonging, identity, in the gratification of our desires through the economic. Whether our hungers are really met in the array which we are invited to consume is debatable. What is sure is that the cost of economic growth is huge, and is unequally borne by the poorest and most vulnerable. The damage to the earth's ecology is already well known, and in the long term renders everyone deeply insecure.

In almost every area of life, from gender roles to the nature of work to the role of religion, this is a time of radical transition, a *kairos*, which demonstrates crisis, a need to choose, which holds both danger and opportunity. In times of transition, when meaning, belonging, identity are all in crisis, there is also radical re-evaluation. Our *values* are shaped by the experiences, people and things that in the past determined meaning, belonging and identity for us. But the focus of values is shifting now from the institutional to the relational. We now increasingly judge, evaluate, decide what something is worth to us, how much it matters, by the quality of relationship it allows and invokes. In a free-market, capitalist philosophy, the criteria for evaluation are extrinsic, they are set by the market. Value is added. The shift to having these as the criteria for relationship is well under way.

But for those people (many, I think) who neither wish to return to the institutional rather than the relational as the matrix of values, nor are able to accept the values of extrinsic worth, this re-evaluation is absolutely crucial. What does it mean to live in right relationship at the end of the millennium? What do values of intrinsic worth look like, and how do they show up? Is this a time for a reappraisal of the nature and significance of land, work, community and religion (and especially, of course, for people who are drawn to the person of Jesus, of the Christian religion)?

Our values show up not so much in what we say or profess, but in what we *care* about and take care of. It is how people know they are valued – that they are cared about, that care is taken in dealing with them. In the past, there was a great deal of inherited wisdom about how to care. But that too has undergone and continues to undergo change. We have moved, for example, from a pattern in which aged and vulnerable people were cared for at home by relatives, through a time when many of them were cared for in residential homes and institutions to the present strategy of 'care in the community'.

Nor is care always to be understood now in the rather paternalistic mode of being taken care of, or helped. People with disability, for example, would more often see care now in terms of empowerment, supporting them in the maximum level of independent living and personal development, rather than in having things done for them. The strands of the web of care – where they are not broken or tangled – are being rewoven in different ways.

And after, 2,000 years of Christianity, the challenge remains as acute as ever of how we care about and live with *difference*. As populations are ever more mobile, different ways of being are constantly coming into closer and closer contact. The challenges of pluralism are the challenges of peace in a world continually at war. Boundaries are constantly breaking down and then re-forming. Who are our allies, across new and old boundaries, and is there a way to engage with those whom we consider to be our enemies other than hostility?

Belonging to the same faith does not protect us from having to deal with difference. We no longer have a Christendom, a Holy Roman Empire, but Christianity extends across the world, and Christians on every continent are exercising the freedom to be located as Christians in their own culture, history and geography. There seem to be more and more stories about what it means to be a Christian, and some of these Christian stories are in direct conflict with each other. How do we in Britain relate to these conflicts? And how do we relate to the people across the world with whom our faith tells us we are intimately connected, as close as the limbs of a body?

And when religion, perhaps particularly the Christian religion, is perceived almost exclusively by those outside it in terms of morality, of right and wrong beliefs, attitudes and conduct, and comes to be judged in these terms, what does it mean to be a Christian for whom faith is not mostly about these things, but is instead about passion, desire, loss, failure, mystery, life, death and the body? Is it still a story for those who sense that the church is only comfortable with the respectable and the 'good', that it is unbending, even ruthless to those who have messy lives?

And at the end of a millennium, in a world scarred by injustice, above all is it still a story that moves us, not just to weep and to pray but to act? Can it make of us sisters and brothers?

'I am a stone' shouted Marta, this dumpy little young woman from El Salvador, rolling up her sleeves, shaking with frustration and pointing her finger in accusation. 'You Europeans must be intentional about working together with us. You must get clear what you are doing. Do you not know that the European Community is an all-out war against the poor? You are out to kill us! But as Christians we are one body, and if one part hurts, the whole body hurts ... is that not what the Bible tells us?'

In the stunned embarrassed silence she went on, 'I need to shake the world to a new reality, and if you are not expecting to shake the world, why are you here? One day the stones are going to speak ... well, here is a stone talking to you ... I am begging you to really listen to us, to read the signs ... unless you really listen to us, you can talk yourselves to sleep.

'While you sleep, my people, in Nicaragua, in El Salvador, in Brazil, in the Philippines, are dying ... there are death squads killing my people.

'I am alive thanks to God, and it is one of the tricks of God that I still call you brothers and sisters. I am bringing you not the helplessness but the hopefulness of the struggling people. We don't need help, we need brothers and sisters in the struggle to change the world.'

(Erik Cramb, *Tayside Industrial Mission Annual Report*, 1990)

2

Into the Unknown?
A Question of Meaning

When I was a child, I was fascinated with maps. I would spend many hours poring over atlases, finding my street on the map of Edinburgh, my city on the map of Scotland, my country on the map of the world. It was another version of the child's instinct to locate herself – I was

Kathryn Orr
2 Caiystane Terrace
Edinburgh 13
Scotland
UK
Europe
The World
The Universe

But it was not just about finding where I was on the map. It was also about imagining all the places I was not, all the places I might one day go. I loved the shapes and colours of the maps, the strange names. Different places engaged my attention as I grew up, reflecting, perhaps, the different influences in my life. At one time, an attachment to movie westerns, and a romantic identification with what we have now learned to call Native North Americans or First Nation people but then simply knew as Red Indians, had me reciting these names with beautiful sounds – Montana, Wyoming, Wisconsin, Connecticut, Manitoba, Saskatchewan. I could trace my literary and cinematic inclinations; from the Chalet School books, beloved of generations of schoolgirls, sending me searching through the Alps for the Austrian Tyrol and the Bernese Oberland, through the frozen expanses of Russia with Dr Zhivago to the streets and districts of Manhattan with Gene Kelly and Henry James and Woody Allen. On the maps were not just geography but history (the Northern Europe of the Reformation, the Scotland of the '15 and the '45), culture, politics, family (here was New Brunswick where my cousin Elaine had emigrated to, and there was Malaya where Uncle Bertie was killed in the war). Even religion was on the map, above all on the map of Africa (here is where David Livingstone discovered the Zambesi – or so we were taught – and Nigeria where Mary Slessor was a missionary...).

But among the maps I loved most, partly because they were like works of art in themselves, were the medieval maps of the world, like the *Mappa Mundi* of Hereford Cathedral. Of course, these maps did not at all resemble the kind we had in school geography lessons. Large parts of the world were not on the map. You would not get very far in a Geography standard grade exam (the Scottish equivalent of GCSEs) if you wrote 'Here lie monsters' in the middle of the Pacific Ocean, as these old maps did. And none of my school maps had God on them.

The early cartographers were pioneers and explorers. They charted places no one had ever done before to extend the area of human knowledge. They found important new information about the land and the seas of the earth. But they did not just convey information. They also interpreted it. They were a bit like editors. Because they could not include every piece of information that is available to the human senses – something like 30,000 separate bits every day – they had to decide what was most important, most significant, to include. And they had to find ways to express what all the information meant. In doing that, all they had was the language and understanding of their time. To take one basic piece of knowledge, they thought the earth was flat – and so other new information was interpreted in the light of this belief. Among the real fears of the early explorers was the fear that they might fall off the edge of the earth.

European medieval world-view put a transcendent God at the centre of its map. And God was on their maps of the world because he (and God was almost always 'he' then) was at the centre of how they understood their lives. Their sense of meaning, what you might call their interior or life-map, their story about life, revolved around God. What was not understood was attributed to the actions of God. What we might see quite clearly today as an illness caused by a virus, they might have seen as a punishment from God; epilepsy might be attributed to possession by devils. God was at the centre of all understanding, action, thought. God was the explanation for everything not understood.

The home territory, on earth at least, of this transcendent God, was known as Christendom, which at different times was synonymous with, or a development of, the Holy Roman Empire. This territory, which, broadly speaking, meant Europe and parts of the Near and Middle East and North Africa, was the 'saved' territory. Within it were Christians. Beyond it were heathens, or even worse, infidels (Muslims) who needed to be 'saved'. There had to be bloody crusades against Islam (which was generally far more tolerant of Christians than Christians were of them); there had to be missionary expeditions to accompany the ruthless colonialist expansionism of European powers into Asia and the Americas. The fact that the European map of the world did not accurately reflect how the rest of the world understood itself – was in fact hugely flawed – was neither here nor there. The Christendom map was the dominant one. It was the right one. At least, it was the right one to further European interests. The height of Eurocentrism was reached in the fifteenth-century Treaty of Tordesillas, when two European powers, Spain and Portugal, divided the unknown world to the East and to the West into two spheres of activity – the ultimate goal of both being the fabled wealth of the East.

But by the eighteenth century the maps were changing. More of the earth's surface had been charted. And the life-map was changing too, at least in the West. Science, reason, logical thought, what could be proved, were seen to be the ways in which things could be explained. And individual freedoms and rights, like the right to vote, were beginning to be important. Nonconformity, religious tolerance, freedom of conscience, all assumed a higher value. The place of God on the map had changed. No longer seen as the explanation of everything not understood, God was still on the map – but seen much more as the judge and guarantor of individual and social morality, bestowing rewards for good behaviour, punishing wrongdoing. The place of God was moving from objective knowledge to subjective ethics.

In the modern era, this has shaped much of our history. It has given us widely held standards of right and wrong, and has been the basis of much valuable social improvement – against slavery, against racism, against poverty and injustice. God has been present on the modern map.

But this map too is changing. Though as a teenager I questioned the authority of church, school, government and particularly my poor mother, with whom I argued for years, it never occured to me to question the accuracy of the maps I was taught with at school. Here was the world, projected by Mercator. I trusted it to be a true description of the earth. After all, it was scientific – it had to be objective! But about twenty-five years ago, a German cartographer called Arno Peters made a new projection. It was made by measuring precisely both the land masses of the earth and their relation to each other. It makes the earth look very elongated, as if it has been stretched out. And what it shows is that the old maps had a clear Eurocentric bias – Europe was drawn larger than it actually is. Even scientists cannot avoid interpreting from the perspective of their own language and culture and self-interest. The interior map is projected on to the exterior one. I once saw a map of the world projected from Australia, with the Pacific in the centre, and I realized how much the way I actually thought about Australia – on the margins, down in the bottom right-hand corner of my inner map – reflected the physical maps I had grown up with. I learned to question all the maps.

And in the life-map too, the bias is there. In the modern era, Europe, the West, has understood itself to be civilized, and those outside it to be primitive, in need of enlightenment. The arrogance of this in a part of the world that has created the savagery of the Somme, Auschwitz and the gulags of the Soviet Union is amazing.

Christianity has also participated in this, and sometimes blessed it. Sometimes the so-called Christian morality has been a way of legitimizing the interests of European countries – in the colonial period, and still today. And the scientific enlightenment that was to save humanity, on the relentless march up the hill called progress, has been equally a double-edged sword. As well as the advances in health, wealth and communications, we now have an unparalleled capacity to kill people in inventive ways, a human society in which the wealth of the minority is built on the poverty of the majority, and a dangerously threatened and polluted natural environment.

We now live in a pluralist world where there are many moralities, which, because they have so often been found wanting, command less and less authority. And the dominant world-view is now the economic one, in which human beings are seen primarily in terms of their economic activity and ability to participate in a global market. The Western capitalist map since the Second World War has projected the West as 'developed', and the rest of the world as either 'underdeveloped' or 'developing'. Other criteria for human development, such as the ability to create sustainable communities, to be creative, to be courageous, to survive with dignity in the face of almost overwhelming odds, are disregarded. Can God be present on this map?

The God-less map

For many, perhaps most people in the West, God is absent from the map of life. God is not their explanation, as in the Middle Ages. Nor is God their guarantor of morality, the judge of their conduct. And certainly the God of the Bible is not a friend to those for whom personal wealth is the chief measure of achievement (though there are still many who are keen to claim the authorization of their personal friend God for their own material aspirations, in a weirdly corrupt Protestant work ethic that ignores the Bible while at the same time idolizing it). But for many, God is simply written out as an irrelevance, a hangover from a different age. And for many more, for whom God is still an idea that at least holds a certain power, the awful horrors of life – the charnel-house that is Rwanda, the hell of all the Bosnias, the tragic anguish of a Dunblane, or the crucifixion beyond words of two little girls dying slowly in a Belgian cellar – evoke the plain outraged cry, 'If there is a God, where the hell is he?'

It is this cry that for me makes an important link between the idea of the absence of God in the life-map of Western society and the experience of God's absence in the life of the individual. That cry of absence, 'My God, my God, why have you abandoned me?' (Psalm 22.1) is above all a personal cry, as it was for Jesus (Matthew 27.46), as it was for the people who cried it over and over again in the Psalms. It is a cry which says, 'Why have you torn up my map and left me alone and terrified in this black place?'

It is the cry of a man who said he was the Son of God.

Of course, there are still maps from which God is not absent, maps in which God figures very firmly. They are the theological maps, the maps which seek to interpret life in a way which includes the possibility of God. They too have their own starting points, projected from where they are.

Some theological maps start from the Bible. They seek meaning and truth, they study writings and texts, they use methodologies of reason and critique and dialogue. They are primarily developed in academies, universities and colleges. They draw a map for belief.

Some theological maps are projected from the church. They seek beauty and order, they draw on tradition and dogma, they lean on liturgy and church practice, have been developed in monasteries, seminaries, institutes, church councils. They draw a map for devotion.

And some theologies are projected from experience, from *praxis* (practice), especially from the experience of exclusion. They seek justice, learn by doing, and reflecting on their action. They give especial weight to the experience of the poor and marginalized, are developed in streets and homes and the public arena. They draw a map for liberation.

There have always been these starting points, and at times they have seemed to be extremely polarized, or identified with one part of Christianity. Biblical theologies have traditionally been identified with Protestantism, church theologies with Roman Catholicism and Orthodoxy, for example. But such categories have never been entirely accurate; biblical theologies have needed churches to authorize them, church theologies have had their own biblical theologies, and liberation theologies, drawing heavily on biblical stories, have grown from a radical critique of churches of different denominations.

Cultural context has also shaped the theological maps. A biblical theology may be very different according to whether it is being done in North America, Southern Africa or South India. Church theology in Egypt will have many different features from that of Poland. Liberation theology takes different shapes done by indigenous peoples in the Pacific, women in the Caribbean or the lesbian and gay community in Britain.

And today those who would be theological map-makers, those who would chart what it means to live with God on the map at the approach of a new millennium, are faced once again with the question of how to select the features of real significance, and how to order the signs and symbols in this time, 'so as to make of the welter a world that will last'. In this task, it is not enough to pore over the old maps, wailing because people will not follow them, or trying to present them in new and glossy colours. It is not enough simply to be a map-maker: it is also necessary to be an explorer, or at least to listen attentively to those people who have travelled where the maps do not go.

We need to listen to the people who take on the challenge of fundamentalism, of whatever brand, which says, 'There is only one map, and it's ours, and it's right, and if you don't follow it you'll be lost for all eternity.'

And we need to listen to the people who take on the challenge of pluralism, of many maps for the same territory, at least some of which may have some signposts for our confusion.

We need to listen to the people who challenge the still hugely powerful map of modernism, which says, 'The map of expansive material progress is the best one, to which there is no real alternative, and anyway we know what's best for you.'

And we need to listen to the people who take on the challenge of postmodernism which says, 'All maps are socially constructed in someone's interest, to exert control, therefore you can't trust any of them. In fact, it's a waste of time even thinking about maps.'

Every kind of exploration carries within it both threat and opportunity, and the only certainty is of exposure to vulnerability. This is not a safe option. And perhaps the greatest challenge is to discover the common ground between the map where God is present and the one where God is absent.

Perhaps a touching place, a place where the tips of our outstretched fingers just meet, is in that cry of Jesus on the cross, 'My God, my God, why have you abandoned me?' The cry of abandonment, of desolation, shows up on both maps. I think it does that, whether it is expressed in terms that include God or not, because it is a cry that does not actually belong to the maps. It is a cry that belongs to the ground of human experience.

For me and, I suspect, for most people, a personal cry demands a personal response. A personal response is not necessarily an individual response. A personal response is one that responds to our need as persons. A hungry man will not be filled by someone telling him his food-growing land is needed to grow coffee to generate cash for foreign debt repayments. Someone who has just lost a loved one does not need reasons, they need a hug or someone to do the shopping. In my experience, not many people in distress are helped by an idea, however beautiful or theologically or politically correct.

I cannot rest my faith on God as explanation. I am a product of the modern era, and I believe in rational thought, democracy, liberty of conscience and the pursuit of knowledge, though not at all costs. My belief in them is not absolute – some of them have the potential to become idols, false gods. But I do not find God present in a set of religious propositions either. That map has been torn up for me.

Nor does my faith rest on God as moral judge, ethical guarantor. Though I am passionate about justice, about right relationship, God is not present for me in morality. As Paul takes unceasing pains to point out, morality, a society's rules about what is right and what is wrong, is inadequate to deal with the profoundest questions of good and evil, life and death. In a world of intolerable injustice, Christianity has increasingly come to mean for me what happens when morality runs out.

When the maps do not extend to the place you find yourself in, the overwhelming experience is of abandonment, of the absence of God. Sometimes it takes that kind of lostness to discover that it is a very limited kind of faith if you have got a map. When you do not have a map, either you can stay where you are, or you can decide to trust the ground, to step out on it, not knowing where you are going, or what dangers await you. In my experience of lostness, God became a real presence to me only through incarnation, by people and things that carried the word made flesh in very material, specific ways.

Not the map but the ground

God was and is present for me only as God on earth: in watching the great life cycle of birth and death and regeneration in a single tree outside my window over the course of a year, and seeing in that single tree the whole pattern of reality; in some people whose courage and humour in the face of grinding injustice kicked my ego off its throne at the centre of the universe and put it in a more realistic place; in discovering that what sometimes seems like the somewhat sadistic weight of working and washing and cooking is actually part of the regenerative flow of life; in the person who gave me a hug and said 'I love you' when I felt utterly unlovable. Over and over again God is represented on earth and, like so many people, including people with far more experience of abandonment than me, I found that, for me, God is not the map, God is the ground. In the words of Isaiah, written two and a half thousand years ago, I discovered the rock from which I came, the quarry from which I was dug (see Isaiah 51.1).

For all their appeal, there are some maps that need to be torn up. The map that says we've got God on our side; or that God hates Catholics – or Jews, or Hindus, or Muslims, or whoever. One of the reasons that the medieval map with God at the centre was torn up was in large part because people had got so sickened by the brutal and interminable religious wars of the sixteenth and seventeenth centuries that for their sheer survival they had to adopt new modes of liberty and tolerance. One might say they had to rescue God from being misrepresented. God has been made present to me as often by Muslims and atheists as by Christians.

And the Bible is full of stories about people who learned the meaning of faith when their maps were torn up – a faith that walks rather than one that talks. Abraham, Moses, Ruth, Mary, Paul, Jesus himself on the cross. They discovered God present when they took the risk of trusting in God even when God was absent for them.

The absence of God is a constant feature of history from the Exodus to the Holocaust, from the slaughter of the Canaanites to the slaughter of Hiroshima, because it is our description of the experience of abandonment and death. For me, the presence of God is understood in the experience of the life that comes out of death, and therefore I trust above all the Incarnation of Jesus, the word made flesh. For me, the cross is the identification of God with the powerlessness of death. For me, the resurrection is both the promise and the power that God gives to bring life out of death, which is the promise and power of love. So for me, the women who went beyond the maps to rescue Moses, and Peter's response to Jesus at Caesarea Philippi, and the person who said, I love you, and the woman whose child had been murdered who campaigned against the death penalty are not divided, and in a mysterious but quite material way they are part of Jesus and held for me by Jesus. They make the word flesh, they step out on faith, they represent God. And through them, it was in the absence of God that I found God most present, most near, right where I was, on the ground.

Rabbi Lionel Blue says that the only power God has in the world is the love he inspires in us. For me, this is the meaning of the incarnation. I could say that for me the story of Jesus encompasses and symbolizes the meaning of life. The 'yes' I found myself saying at the age of fifteen on reading Whitman's poem, not as to something new, but with all the force of recognition, is named for me within the life of Jesus. The conviction of the intrinsic worth of all that exists, the conviction of the relatedness of all things, the conviction of the miraculousness of the ordinary, all exist within the Christian story, compellingly enough for me to step out on it. These are the features of real significance that I have selected.

And of course, in so doing I am drawing a map, projected from my experience and observation and influences, good and bad, from where my feet touch the earth. In my engagement with the Christian story, I edit, I select, I interpret. Now, this admission is the kind that causes hysteria among dogmatic map-makers of any persuasion, who would prefer to maintain the illusion that they have the infallible map, which is absolutely pure and good and true and devoid of editorializing. They would prefer that we simply accept that this is the way things are, 'Here is the nine o'clock news'.

Thundering of the dangers of moral relativism or consumer religion or pick-and-mix philosophies may well make them feel better, stronger, more powerful perhaps. And as T. S. Eliot said famously, 'Human beings cannot bear very much reality.' But to imagine that the human search for meaning has ever been anything else than a process which selects and edits is delusory, a negation (for a start) of the life of Christ, of the canon of the Bible and of 2,000 years of Christian history. And it is simply not realistic to think that 'because I/we/they say so' is adequate for most people today, whatever their beliefs.

Of course maps can be imposed. Of course people can be coerced or frightened or seduced or just plain bullied into accepting them. But it is a self-defeating exercise. Then it is not about meaning, far less truth. Then it is simply about power. And human beings go on maddeningly reserving to themselves the right to think their own thoughts.

And as I project my map, marked as it is by convictions about life which are shared by many who are not Christian, and are not shared by many who are, I am already displaying some of the influences, experiences and biases which have shaped the processes by which I construct that map. Some of these are not peculiar to me – the experience of being a woman, for example, I have in common with slightly more than half the human race. But the experience of being a woman in Britain at the end of a century which has seen unparalleled changes in what that involves has undoubtedly shaped my particular and specific story hugely. Other experiences are less general, some are entirely personal. But they are never entirely individual; for my map is not just geography, it is not just gender, it is history and culture and politics and community, it is desire and loss, wound and gift. You can read all of these on my map.

For a number of reasons, many of which will show up in other chapters of this book, I am a religious person, by which I mean I am someone who understands the universe as humanly meaningful. Therefore, although many of the old maps hold no meaning for me, it still seems a worthwhile thing to attempt to construct new maps, new templates, while recognizing that all our projections are at best provisional. In this, I am one of many.

A few years ago I went to see Kenneth Branagh's film version of *Much Ado About Nothing*, and sat in the cinema as the whole audience became caught up in the enchantment of what the Scottish film critic Joyce McMillan described as 'the life-enhancing exuberance of it all'. We laughed, we sighed, we were delighted, and once again the powerful myth of romantic love worked its magic, even on a cynical 1990s Glasgow audience.

But all the way through it, I was aware that much of the attraction of the film did not lie just in the romance or the sparkling dialogue or the beauty of the language and acting. It lay equally in the beautiful Tuscan setting, in the harmonious simplicity of a pleasant communal life, in the sense of natural abundance without excess, and in the sharpened focus and awareness of life, of a community poised for a moment of respite and release between two wars. Take away the communal context, set the film in some dank slum or some isolated great house with only its aristocratic owners, and much of the magic would have been lost. But as it was, it was a demonstration of what Joyce McMillan called 'the common stuff of life linked confidently to a whole order of the universe; the deep hard-won richly-patinaed joy that came from the simultaneous fulfilment of individual needs, and those of a whole society'.

That picture is, in itself, perhaps a romantic one; how often did the collective ordering of the universe actually manage to do these two things? But there is still a yearning for its possibility. The myth, the map of romantic love, is pretty fragile these days; divorce rates might suggest it is crumbling. The fact that our happiness now seems to have a thin quality – it lacks social resonance, is a private matter – permanently excludes so many from the possibility of the happy ending. But as this particular myth crumbles, without some other, equally powerful, equally erotic vision, then people, even young people, are left with the sense that there is no shape, no point, no purpose to life. This void becomes a breeding ground for less inclusive, more dangerous forms.

> And the point about all this – the shapelessness, the cynicism, the entropy, the rejection of old dreams, the inability to develop new ones – that it is not sustainable. Human beings crave meaning and need dreams. We need to know what to hope for, and very few are loners enough to draw the whole map for themselves. The rest of us like to feel part of some rhythm, some order of things, and the more we mouth the inadequate rhetoric of 'do your own thing' and 'it's nobody else's business', the greater becomes the danger of a hysterical lurch-back towards a sexual politics that is strict, secure, authoritarian and ultimately fascistic.
> (Joyce McMillan)

I think this is true not just in our sexual politics.

> ... but what I wanted to know was,
> where is honour?
> because everywhere I looked, I saw betrayal.

> I thought if I went away, somewhere entirely new,
> I would find it,
> among people who were heroic, who knew how to live.

> I looked among people who lived close to the elements,
> who loved the spareness of rock and water
> and remembered legends,
> but betrayal was there, coiling into the rock,
> heaving under the water.

> So I looked again, among the people who lived by law
> and aspired to righteousness,
> but betrayal had got there before me
> and was feasting on the vitals of the served-up.

> But 'there are lovers, there must be lovers' I thought,
> shattering death with their undying passion.
> That was the worst country.

I fell into a long darkness of despair.
There was no ground of honour.

Then it came to me.
To have the search was to have the ground.
I remembered that, where there was betrayal,
there was also love;
before, beside, after.

It was enough.
I turned, and headed for home.

(KG, from an unpublished play)

3

No Life without Roots?
A Question of Belonging

The Scottish journalist Kenneth Roy once described a visit he made to an island in the Outer Hebrides of Scotland, to a remote village where daily life was hard, if not any longer as grinding as it had been, and where the local history had been marked by a number of fishing tragedies of the kind that desolate small, close communities. He joined the local Free Church congregation for worship, and here, in a liturgy bereft of any relief of colour, movement or visual imagery, plain in the extreme, he found himself addressed by what he termed 'the unbearable fact of God'. The austerity of the worship reflected that of the landscape itself: barren, rocky, battered by Atlantic gales, where little grows in thin soil and the harvest of the sea is hard won, and yet with a stark beauty in its simplicity and quality of light.

It is for me a powerful image of the way in which our environment interacts with our self-understanding. Does a particular habitat create its own meaning, predisposing its inhabitants to interiorize and signify their external surroundings? Could such an austere religious landscape exist in a similar way in the gentle wooded slopes and fertile valleys of southern England, for example? Or is meaning sought to make some kind of sense of the particularities of place? The inhabitants of an even bleaker island, St Kilda, many miles off the north coast of Scotland, believed that the illnesses, poverty and hardship they suffered, and the tragic loss of so many babies at birth (actually caused by bad midwifery practices), was punishment from God because they were 'a wicked generation'.

We know that before they ever have language, babies perceive the world through their senses, bombarded with sensory messages in

28

every moment of every day. As language and relationship with the people in their environment develops, some of that early sensory awareness is dulled. But the sense of place, of surroundings, that is a significant factor in our interpretation of the world has its roots in some of our first experiences. It lays foundations for our relationship to our location, whether we will like it or not, whether it nurtures us or not, whether we have a feeling of belonging in it, or one of alienation. It affects our response to such concepts as 'nature' and 'land' and 'home'. A sense of place is one of the most profound human experiences. For many people, it is stronger than their attachment to other human beings. It is part of what motivates patriotism, nationalism, artistic expression, religious devotion, ecological concern and personal and political identity.

This century, and especially the last twenty years or so, has seen an increased ecological awareness worldwide. From concern about global warming to the pollution of lakes, the destruction of rainforests and the threat to bio-diversity all the way to concern about localized eco-systems, the fate of the earth, in its unity and in its diversity, has moved up the public agenda. We have begun to realize that our habitat is indivisible, that what affects one part ultimately affects all parts, that 'when one part of the body suffers, all the other parts suffer with it' (1 Corinthians 12.26). No longer tied to old concepts of dead matter, we know that we inhabit a living earth.

This increasing awareness is changing our maps. Our geography is in constant transition. And our interior geography is also shifting. But the maps are not all the same. There are many attitudes to what we call 'nature', or our habitat, our earth with its universe. They can include:

- nature as a resource to be managed;
- nature as an opportunity to be exploited;
- nature as a potential to be developed;
- nature as an aesthetic to be appreciated;
- nature as the stage on which human destiny is worked out;
- or simply, nature as a nice surrounding in which to take exercise, conquer mountains or escape the pressures of modern living.

All of these are *attitudes of extrinsic worth*. That is to say, they add value to nature in terms of its desirability to the human race, though some of them may seem more benign than others, and may include a love or enjoyment of nature.

Others are *attitudes of intrinsic worth*. These have different names: the Green movement, deep ecology, creation spiritualities. They have different origins and different expressions. They include:

- indigenous or aboriginal traditions and communities;
- followers of pagan religion;
- some movements or groups within the historical world religions, such as Zen Buddhism, Hindu, Yoga, Sufi mysticism, the Jewish Cabbala, and, in Christianity, the rediscovery and re-evaluation of the insights and practices of Celtic Christianity, of the Rhineland mystics and the Franciscans, along with the growth of modern movements within all the religions;
- what might be called a scientific spirituality, motivated in study and research by the intrinsic beauty, complexity and awesomeness of the universe;
- groups within what is loosely titled the New Age movement, though not all New Age groups demonstrate such attitudes;
- perhaps most numerous, those individuals and groups who would not place themselves in any of these categories, but who are simply people for whom and to whom the universe speaks in the language of love, and who respond with love and respect and the desire for natural justice.

These categories do not have rigid boundaries, and there is considerable overlapping between them. But they share a dominant common characteristic. Their profound motivation is one of respect and reverence for the forms and elements and species of the earth because they have intrinsic value, and because we are connected to them, a species among species, programmed to adapt and survive.

A species among other species. Though we may have an intellectual awareness of this in our society, it is somewhat difficult to take it on board. Even with a deep conviction of intrinsic worth, we still have problems of perspective, and the pressures to disconnect are acute.

We recognize the fact that indigenous or aboriginal cultures often have highly evolved ways of living in right relationship with their habitat. These ways are highly unitive, deeply connective. They have lived in what anthropologists have termed a 'participation mystique' of undivided wholeness in which even the term 'reverence for nature' is inaccurate because it conveys rather too much 'over-againstness' for a context in which such a degree of differentiation has not been conceived of.

The experience of uprootedness

But such cultures who have been torn up by the roots from the land on which they grew by the forces of what is sometimes rather misleadingly called 'progress' or 'development' are forced into a brutal differentiation which is almost unimaginable for us in our highly individualistic culture. Western cultures have had centuries of this brutalization. We have been torn up by the roots so often. This is part, for example, of what it means to be Scottish.

Ask a group of Scots to locate themselves on the map of Scotland, and then ask them to pinpoint where their greatgrandparents lived, and the demographic patterns and trends of the last 150 years show up very clearly. The industrial Central Belt of Scotland dragged people in from the rural areas, the Highlands, the islands, the borders, the south-west, like a magnet, in the process of urbaniza-tion that the break-up of the clan system, the Highland Clearances and the Industrial Revolution brought with them. Our geography shows our history. The map of Scotland simply shows on a smaller scale what has gone on across the world since, and is still going on today: the destruction of older forms of community, deforestation and the degradation of habitats, the introduction of cash cropping (of which sheep and deer in the Highlands are an early example – in other parts of the world it could be coffee or tobacco) on to formerly food-growing land, brutal land-clearance, population growth and the movement to urban centres in search of waged work by people who had previously lived by land and exchange.

But the processes that sucked people in to the industrial centre also spat them out to the other side of the world.

Others in that group of Scots will have family connections in Australia, New Zealand, South Africa, the United States and, above all, in Canada. The exodus of particularly Highland Scots across the Atlantic to Canada was huge, to the extent that today the map of Canada is dotted with Scottish placenames; the migrants from Scotland, homesick and heartsick, called these strange new places after the dear places they had left behind. The city of Calgary, for example, was settled in by Scots from a remote corner of the north of the Hebridean island of Mull. And today there are more native Gaelic speakers in Nova Scotia, 'New Scotland', than there are in the whole of Scotland. Ask the same group of Scots to mark on a map of the world where they now have relatives and other trends become apparent. Some of them will have part of their families in Italy, in Poland, in China. Some will have them in Pakistan and India. Many will have them in Ireland. These are the people who migrated to Scotland in successive waves over the last century. Their cultures, traditions, gifts, are part of what makes Scotland the country it is today.

These people, the ones who came to Scotland and the ones who left it, were overwhelmingly economic migrants. They were not escaping from religious or political persecution, they came and went because they were cleared out, burned out, starved out; because their land was exhausted, because it was more profitable for landlords to keep sheep than people, because they were superfluous to the needs of their country's economy. It is ironic that having offered surplus people cheap passages across the seas in order to get rid of them, our current immigration and asylum laws are extremely hostile to economic migration. 'Do as we say, not as we do.'

So many uprooted people! Our routes are also our roots. The music and literature and drama of Scotland echo with the cries of people uprooted: the songs of exile and yearning, the stories of displacement and alienation, the theatre trying to reconstruct meaning in the urban experience.

I write from my own context, a Scottish one, but of course the experience of displacement, of the search for roots, is a global one.

It seems to me to be one of the great gifts of being part of a religious tradition that there are scriptures, ceremonies, music and stories that remind us of our roots, of times when we were not so disconnected. The biblical story of the Exodus describes the experience of the early Israelites through origins, exile, wandering in the wilderness and arrival in the promised land. It is a particular story, its geography can be located on the map, its history in specific chronology. But its vivid recollection of a people through generations of leaving and arriving, struggle and wandering, hope and captivity, and its attempt to discern meaning in and through all of it, have a wider resonance. The Exodus story has been meaningful for dispossessed and exiled people across the world: black slaves in North America and landless *campesinos* in Brazil have identified with the human experience described by the whole notion of exodus. The Scots going to their new world sang the exilic psalms of the Israelites because they were true to their experience; they too shared the ambivalence of the 'promised land'.

As an expression of interior disposession and exile, the Exodus also speaks powerfully. For groups of people in Scotland, words come easily to describe the experience of home, exile, wilderness, promised land. To move from the safety, shelter, clear identity, recognition, warmth of being 'at home' to the loss, alienation, isolation, lack of identity of exile is immediately recognizable for someone who has just been bereaved, or been exiled from the world of work through forced redundancy. To wander in the wilderness of confusion, exposure, vulnerability, lack of control, no signposts, is what it is like for many people who have just been diagnosed with cancer or as HIV positive.

And to find other meanings in these experiences is also a journey of faith, where arrival has no guarantees. To discover the different perspectives and opportunities and interdependencies of exile; the new sense of identity, the wider horizons, the grace of survival in the wilderness, is also to face a re-evaluation of the old loyalties, securities and certainties of the place of origination. And deeper questionings about the nature of the 'promised land' return us once again to the maps: how much does the vision of the promised land involve exclusion or disposession? Indigenous peoples, like the First Nation people of Canada, may identify more clearly with the disposessed Canaanites of the Bible. And will we recognize our promised land if we get there? Arrival too can be a loss, resurrection a terrifying possibility.

And yet there is a sense in which the meaning of the promised land is only possible for us through memory and hope, because of the powerful reminder of what we have lost, or know we never had but always longed for – a place of belonging.

COMING HOME

When you cross the borders of the desert
and head for home
you do not want to turn back.
What you are heading for is a place of belonging
a place where you can lay your body down.
Everything inside you is running
you have run away often
but this time you are running for home.

You will still be yourself
still be restless sometimes and afraid
but what beckons you now are bonds of loving
and, when all is said and done,
(and sometimes there is too much saying and too little doing)
living where your life belongs is coming home.
Welcome to the family.

(Ruth Burgess, 1996)

This poem was written for someone joining the church. Still at the end of the twentieth century, it is truly part of the Christian story that for many people, uprooted, alienated, shut out, the church, the Christian community, has been a place of homecoming, the place where their lives belong. Here, they have been able to put down new roots.

Uprooted, it is harder for us to know ourselves as a species among species. In our religious faith, there may also be a strong unitive, connective concern, self-consciously so, one we strive for, whether it be in an undifferentiated absorption into the divine or Godhead, or whether, as in Christianity, in the belief that the fullest realization of selfhood or differentiation comes in union with God. But if one part of religion is the attempt to conceive of the universe as humanly meaningful, there is also the temptation to interpret that as meaning that humankind is what the universe is for. And thence, it is only a small step to the arrogance of believing that the universe is for us – of making ourselves the value-adders to creation. So it may be a considerable struggle to affirm that, on the contrary, we are for the universe.

Both in our relationship with our own habitat and in our relationship with God the sociological and historical pressures running against connectedness are acute. And though a scientific spirituality may have a clearer picture of our ecological interdependence, it is still subject to the pervasive and persuasive strategy of making the end justify the means, in a value-loaded, anthropocentric way – as conflicts about everything from animal-testing to nuclear power demonstrate.

And then, even if relatedness to the creation and all its complex bio-diversity is simply that of the passionate lover whose ultimate concern is the well-being of the beloved earth, there always and genuinely exists the claims of another or other loves. Sometimes the choices and demands seem irreconcilable. Perhaps this is seen most acutely in the dilemma of those who cut wood for fuel, in order just to survive, in the full knowledge that they are destroying part of the biological foundation of their own life on earth. Anyone who has found themselves with apparently competing loves is aware of the anguish of this struggle.

Being a species among species, recognizing our connections, also means recognizing our finiteness, our contingency, our limits. This presents certain huge problems to Western cultures living with economic and political ideologies that are, after all, the logical conclusion of the Enlightenment, that movement which brought many gifts, some of them poisoned. We live in a society which entices with limitlessness, and offers the promise of escape from the demands of finiteness. Both personally and politically, on the left and on the right, our society entices us to disengage from the confines and demands and limitations of history, of geography, of bodies, of relationship. We repress, distort, deny our history, the hurts done both to us and by us. We attempt to leap over geography in our cars and planes, cause carnage on the roads and poison the atmosphere. We systematically demean, degrade, armour and hurt bodies. We pay lip service to community, live out of individualism, and pay to find ways of recreating spurious community.

Speaking recently, Jonathan Porritt, searching for the reasons why people do not take ecological issues seriously now, said,

> Simply, not enough people are dying yet in our countries; of skin cancer, of UV rays, or from pollution toxification illnesses. Nor are enough coastal communities drowning yet from rising sea-levels due to global warming. The visible, tangible, avoidable consequences of ecodisaster are not yet powerful enough to persuade sufficient people to change today's priorities.

Is this what we are headed for in the West? Is our denial of reality so great, our denial of our finitude, and the planet's finitude so strong that, having rolled back our boundaries so firmly over other people and species, having externalized our costs to such a degree, we have lost the ability to self-limit, and must wait for the limitations laid upon us by catastrophe and tragedy? Certainly, the failure at the 1997 Kyoto Summit on Climate Change of some of the world's richest countries, notably the United States of America, to fulfil promises made at the 1992 Earth Summit in Rio de Janeiro to reduce greenhouse gas emissions seems to suggest so.

'Free thinker, do you think you are the only thinker on this earth, in which life blazes inside all things? Your liberty does what it wishes with the powers it controls, but when you gather to plan, the universe is not there.' If our earth, our habitat, is precious to us, both personally and politically, both globally and locally, what does it really mean to look after the home, to be environmentally friendly?

Living on the land

'The land' is a powerfully evocative term for Scots, as it is for all cultures. It holds many meanings and resonances for people. Perhaps its three most commonly held meanings are:

- the political meaning of land: land as nationality or nation state, as in 'homeland', 'native land';
- the economic meaning of land: land as property, utility, resource, commons, as in 'land-owning', 'landless';
- the cultural meaning of land: land as countryside, nature, as in 'landscape'.

On the basis of these commonly held meanings for 'land', significant numbers of people are excluded who are not actively participant in any of these categories. And yet at a more basic level it is a false exclusion. We all live on the land, we all place our feet on ground, terra firma, whether urban, rural, or the vaguer categories in between which the word 'suburban' does not adequately describe. A healthy relationship between land and people is one based on inclusion, not exclusion.

Environmental concern is not, for many people, first and foremost about the countryside, about wilderness areas and ski-paths, about forestation and fishery protection. But that does not mean either that they are not concerned about the environment, or that they do not care about the countryside. It does mean that they are concerned about *their* environment, the land upon which they live and move and have their being, the environment in which their children will grow up, and which will shape their well-being, aspirations and responsiveness to change and challenge.

That means that those people (who may include us) show up being concerned about exactly the same issues as people in what we traditionally think of as the environmental movement – about jobs, energy use, pollution, transport policies, housing policies and the nature of democracy. In all of these issues, people are struggling with questions of value.

We take care of what we value. Our values show up in what we do, rather than in what we say (as pollsters are always finding to their confounding). I live in the West End of the city of Glasgow, in a friendly environment. A few years ago, I heard an ecologist make a very good case for it as a paradigm of green urban living – tenement houses, solidly built and energy-efficient, good public transport, excellent small local shops, schools, services, parks, entertainments, sports facilities, hospitals – a neighbourhood where places of work, living, service and recreation are integrated in a multicultural environment. And indeed, it is a good place to live. In such a place, community responsibility and ecological concern are very high. People are always cleaning up the river Kelvin, campaigning about the use of the parks, and the maintenance of the public spaces; every street has its residents' association. People value their environment, so they take care of it, and find it takes care of them. They experience it as friendly. It meets their needs. We take care of what we value.

But why do we value what we value? To a great extent, we value what in turn values us – what meets our needs, what affirms us in our life and aspirations, what gives us enjoyment and delight. This is a kind of symbiotic process – we know it with our friends, with our children; if we are fortunate, we know it with our work. It's not usually easy to tell, and probably it does not matter too much anyway, which came first, the valuing or the being valued. They reinforce one another. I think one can make a very good case for people in the West End of Glasgow living in a symbiotic relationship with their environment, with their land, if you like. The environment is friendly to them, so they are friendly back. They take care of it. They invest time and energy and talents, and often money, in it – all of which makes the environment even more friendly. I use an urban example, but there are as many rural ones available.

But what if your environment is not friendly? What if your environment is deeply and implacably hostile? What does this mean for notions of value and care? The extraordinary thing to me is not how few people care about the land – that land whereon they live – but how many still do, against all the odds.

I want to think about how significant numbers of people are excluded from current debates and decision-making about the land because of the kind of understandings we carry about the word. This exclusion cannot, I believe, be easily categorized into a rural/urban split. Many, perhaps most, 'green' campaigners in our society live in urban contexts. And the kind of 'green' activities that go on in the West End of Glasgow and many other urban environments are easily recognized and accommodated under an environmental label. The exclusion is more complex than that. I would like to look at exclusion with reference to two different kinds of lowland community – to peripheral housing schemes, and to post-industrial central-belt town communities. And I want to do it by reference to the meanings with which we usually invest the word 'land'.

Firstly, there is the *political meaning*, the identification of 'land' with the country, the nation state: for me, the land of Scotland. The uses of the word in this way are so familiar they scarcely need mentioning – it is our 'native land', 'the land of our birth', or, it may be, 'our adopted land'. Scots have a powerful myth or story of loving our land, by which we symbolize our geography, our particular reference points on the map. It's an attractive myth; it removes us from a racist identification of nationality with ethnicity; it may include people, but only in the sense of those for whom it is habitat, not in the sense of race. But almost unbidden, the images that come to us about Scotland, and certainly those reinforced in media, advertising and much popular culture, are either of the countryside – mountains, lochs, rivers, shorelines – or of the acceptable faces of urban Scotland – Edinburgh Castle, the Burrell Museum, the old towns. They are less likely to be of Harthill, Easterhouse or Cardenden, of peripheral housing estates and post-industrial towns, unlesss we happen to come from one of these places. It is hard for us to avoid calling up these images. When we want to make a positive identification with something, we select the positive images that will reinforce the identification. They are the ones that give us pride in our land.

But what if you live in a place which has, for whatever reason, a negative image? The pull towards excision, towards exclusion, is powerful. Almost unconsciously, we begin to excise, to exclude Easterhouse or Moss Side or St Paul's from the image of the land that we love. It is not valued. It is harder to care about. People in Easterhouse know this. They are not stupid. The homeless people in Glasgow who were excluded from George Square (the city's main square where they gather for the nightly soup run) during the city's Year of Culture knew this. Their environment did not value them. They were a blot on the landscape.

People in every kind of community in Scotland have shared the experience of political powerlessness over the last twenty years. They have felt the same kind of frustration at the increasing centralization of government, at the erosion of democracy from local accountable bodies into the patronage of quangos, the same sense of being politically marginalized. But there is marginal and marginal. There is the marginality of having one's voice overruled, shouted down or simply ignored. And then there is the marginality of having one's voice silenced, of having to bite back the words so many times that eventually one's throat becomes choked. It becomes impossible to speak. This is part of the experience not just of a dozen years of political frustration, but of decades of powerlessness.

There are parts of Glasgow where the turnout in local government elections is only just into double figures. Whole communities have effectively ceased to participate in the democratic process (in so far as our political system encourages participation). This is not a question of wicked Tory governments who do not care about Scotland. This is a much longer-standing malaise. These are areas which routinely return Labour candidates. In these safe areas, without effective alternatives, people's votes have had little value, have been taken for granted. And then, at the very point at which the political climate started to change, at which the Labour Party stopped undervaluing its support, its own ability to be effective was sharply reduced by legislation constraining local government. It remains to be seen, and it is a huge political challenge, how far the election of a Labour government with a large majority, and the establishment of a devolved Scottish Parliament with wide-ranging powers can reverse this malaise. And this is not just a Scottish phenomenon. We have become familiar recently with the notion of the swing-vote whereby the voting patterns in a few key marginal constituencies are the ones which win and lose elections, and therefore must be courted. Others can largely be taken for granted, and so, in a strict political sense, become irrelevant.

First proposition: in the political meaning of land, where land is identified with nation, there are communities which are symbolically undesirable and politically irrelevant. Excised from consciousness, they are of no value in the political landscape. Their environment does not value them.

If we consider the second meaning of 'land', land as property, possession, asset, utility or resource, a meaning which is primarily *economic*, the sense of exclusion becomes more acute. Take a town like Bellshill. At the heart of the Central Belt, the land on which Bellshill stands has been through a number of metamorphoses. First it was agricultural land. Then it supported a weaving industry. Then it was coal-mining land. The pits closed. Then it was a steel town, two miles from Ravenscraig. Now, steel is finished in Bellshill. Part of that land is Strathclyde Country Park. And the new hope for new jobs on this land, apart from tourism and leisure, lies in distribution businesses. Grounds for hope – perhaps. But somebody in the personnel department of the biggest plant in the area told me that all applications for work are routinely checked first of all for date of birth. If the applicant is over forty years old, the application is immediately put in the bin. For a large percentage of the population of this town, the definitive work experience is of redundancy, sometimes running through generations, only to be faced with the final indignity of being too old at forty.

In the economic landscape of Britain, there are a number of ways of being a stakeholder, which, of course, offer a different size of stake, and of power. You can be an owner, a developer or a manager of land, or a shareholder in any of these. You can be a houseowner. Or you can add value to the land by increasing its utility through the work of your brain or hands, by your skill, experience or muscle. But what if you are excluded from all of these ways of having an economic stake in the land, as many people in Bellshill are? Still, at least in Bellshill, where some people still have work, you can have an economic value as a consumer.

Move to a peripheral scheme, and the picture gets even bleaker. I have a copy of the findings of a research project into the diets of lone-parent and low-income families. Now we all know that the diet in Scotland is considered to be among the worst in the Western world in terms of nutrition and health. This is variously attributed to the bad eating patterns of our society, to ignorance and lack of proper nutritional education, to feckless parenting and to poverty. It certainly cannot be attributed (as it can in other parts of the world) to shortages, lack of natural resources or a poor society generally. The findings of the study relate to inner-city London, but one of the researchers confirmed that the likelihood was that they would be equally applicable to similar groups in Scotland and other parts of Britain.

They find that the main causes of bad eating habits or even

malnutrition are not ignorance (parents are actually remarkably knowledgeable about what constitutes healthy eating) nor lack of care (parents try to privilege their children's diet, and where there is evidence of nutritional deprivation, the parents suffer most), but poverty – firstly in simply not having enough money to buy good food, and secondly because people live in places where access to good quality foodstuffs is severely restricted, and what there is is more expensive. At this point of economic activity, a person has ceased to have even the economic value of being a consumer. One has no market value, therefore no choice, and no consumer clout.

Second proposition: in the economic meaning of land, where land is identified with property, possession, asset, utility or resource, there are communities which are economically redundant, and have absolutely no market value. They are of no value in the economic landscape of Scotland. Their environment does not value them, to the point where their children may be suffering from malnutrition. Furthermore, these communities are most likely to be the ones which are symbolically undesirable and politically irrelevant.

Talk about a hostile environment! Perhaps we are approaching a time when one of the endangered species in Scotland is, quite literally, the children of the poor – as they are on the streets of Rio de Janeiro and the killing fields of Rwanda and the brothels of Bangkok.

And what of the last common meaning of the word 'land'. Perhaps this is the one which has the greatest imaginative power for us – this is land in the sense of 'countryside', 'nature', 'the wild': the places unspoiled by humans, by development, by urbanization, by exploitation. This is a *cultural/spiritual meaning*. It is trees and rivers, shining waters, fresh breezes, the scent of pine, the cry of birds, open skies and not a building in sight. It is deep in our cultural psyche – back to nature, head for the hills, go to the sea. There's a very nice lake in Strathclyde Country Park – it seems natural enough. In fact, its shining waters drowned a number of miners' rows dating back to the last century. Some of its last inhabitants now live in a housing scheme in Bellshill. Once a year they meet at the plaque that marks their homes under the water. Delightful and wholesome though our idea of nature may be, in the lowlands and much of the highlands of Scotland, it's largely fictitious. Trees where there were none, no trees where there were forests, all the work of human hands. There's very little of our 'natural' land that is actually as 'nature' made it. It has simply been developed and diversified in different ways. And what is true in Scotland is more so in other parts of Britain, where 'agribusiness' is much more developed.

The identification of 'land' with 'nature' is intensely problematic when one is thinking about the relationship between land and people, about human ecology. It leads many to think that environmental concern is all about nature, whatever that is. It leads many to think that 'greens' care only about the countryside, and have no interest or concern for those whose habitat is urbanized, or not picturesque. It leads ecology to be seen as an aesthetic.

Third proposition: in the cultural meaning of land, where land is identified with 'nature' or countryside, there are communities which are excluded by being neither, and which, additionally, are seen to possess a kind of negative equity in aesthetics. People in them are considered to be ignorant or uncaring about the environment because of this negative equity. This impression may be reinforced by the suspicion displayed towards environmentalists provoked by a perception of the environmental movement as being uncaring of the environmental well-being of these communities.

To conclude: there are whole communities which are excluded from participation in the environmental debate because they are perceived to be:

- symbolically undesirable;
- politically irrelevant;
- economically redundant;
- aesthetically unattractive;
- environmentally unfriendly.

The tragedy of this exclusion is that it fails to realize the extent of ecological activity that is actually going on in the Bellshills and Easterhouses of Britain. One of the most interesting things about somewhere like North Lanark, grim and post-industrial as it may seem to the outsider, is that, actually, the links between land and people are stronger here than almost anywhere else in Scotland. A recent study found that Lanark has the lowest mobility rates in the country (about 11 per cent). Here are the deepest roots in the land! In a country with little obvious physical beauty, few jobs, much economic hardship, people have an incredible sense of belonging, of loyalty to place. Families go back generations in the one place. Even given better alternatives, people will not necessarily take them. I suspect that the same may be true for the post-industrial communities of the North of England and South Wales.

So what holds people? What gives that sense of belonging? These are areas with a strong recollection of community, with a rich social history and memory. They are often places with a long radical tradition as one of the strands of a history of shared struggle, forged in hard times. And religious history has also given people a sense of value, of being worth caring about. When much of the natural and social environment has been hostile, it has been the communal bonds that have been friendly enough to keep people rooted on their land, holding fast in the relationship, finding civic pride and caring for a physical environment that offers no quick rewards or immediate gratification.

And in the peripheral schemes, there are a great many people who care about the countryside. But their energies are tied up in trying to befriend their own hostile environment, seeking respect from it in the shape of better housing, schools, public transport, policing, rubbish collection; reconnecting person to person in the struggle to re-evaluate not just the physical environment but the social one also, building, or rebuilding a sense of worth within and among communities. It is often the despair of such local neighbourhoods that press, television, theatre, novels all stigmatize them, see only the dilapidation, the drugs, the problems, and are blind to the care, the pride, the problem-solving that actually also goes on. It is a gross insult to the literally millions of our citizens who live in them to describe their homes as 'sink estates', and it does not make it any more palatable that it may be the *Guardian* or the *Independent* doing it. The image of being thrown down the waste pipe is not a friendly one.

If people are to value the land, their land, they need to know it values them. To care for a habitat which is not valued for its political power, which is not economically profitable, which has a negative cultural aesthetic, is to be on the very front line of environmental activism. Such front-line campaigners have already made a spiritual re-evaluation. They have refused the definition of their land in terms of extrinsic worth. They value it as having intrinsic worth. This is an enormous and largely unnoticed and unrewarded investment of value. It is absolutely consistent with the best ecological and religious principles. It should be recognized, affirmed and supported to the hilt. Such recognition, affirmation and support might go some way towards healing the dangerous splits in environmental campaigning. Far from being the villains, or even the passive victims of environmental destruction, poor people and communities are in fact the greatest source of education, resistance and creativity in combating it.

Across the world, in the material and spiritual struggle to find a sense of belonging, to grow deep roots, to be home-makers, it is the poorest who suffer most. It is also the poorest who are the most careful – who recycle rubbish, who do not drive cars or flit around the globe in energy-extravagant jet planes, who drain the least resources, who are resourceful, who go on affirming the intrinsic worth of life – because, given no extrinsic worth, they have to; who know their interdependence, their relatedness, who every day find the glory in the grey.

One of the insights of the Christian story, demonstrated unceasingly in word and action by Jesus, is the necessity of working to get economic and political systems off the backs of the poor, of valuing their immense courage in the Exodus journey to justice and freedom, of learning humility from their resourcefullness and spirit. The extent to which we participate in creating an economic, political and cultural environment which is friendly to the poorest people in our society and our world will be the extent to which all of us can befriend our own environment, our own place. Ultimately, unless we all have a home, a place of belonging, all of our belonging is endangered.

To do this, we need to build new alliances, to sit lightly to our own agendas and our desire to control outcomes, to rediscover the hidden resources and gifts for resistance and re-creation in our own faith and culture. Above all, we need a radical *re-evaluation*.

> the loveliness is everywhere
>> even
> in the ugliest
>> and most hostile environment
> the loveliness is everywhere
>> at the turning of a corner
>>> in the eyes
>> and on the lips
>>> of a stranger
> in the emptiest areas
>> where is no place for hope

and only death
    invites the heart
the loveliness is there
    it emerges
    incomprehensible
     inexplicable
  it rises in its own reality
and what we must learn is
    how to receive it
  into ours

(Kenneth White, 'Extract XV' from 'A Walk along the Shore', 1974)

4

Knowing Me, Knowing You?
A Question of Identity

I used to live in a place where everyone
had been decanted.
(Funny word.
Did it mean we were like wine?)
Slum clearance, new hopes, high houses.
We used to hang around the chip-shop,
go into the woods and fool about,
wander the streets.
I liked it.
In that place,
I walked by flaming torches
and there was crisp snow underfoot
and people hung out of their windows
to hear us singing.

I used to live in a place
where the toilet was on the stair,
the putrid smell of the horsehair factory choked the air
and, some Saturdays, junior Orange Walkers wakened me from sleep
with the sound of hatred made indescribable by its innocence.
In that place,
I saw three boys
beat the Asian owner of the corner shop
with an iron bar
to the pavement.

I used to live in a house above a pub
and sometimes in the morning
there was blood on the tiles
from the stabbing of the night before.

Food was cheap, and men were
always getting laid off, and
violence lay close to the skin, always
ready to erupt like a red stain at the
slightest scratch.
In that place,
I heard a girl scream, and
saw a man rush from a close-mouth doing
up his trousers, and the girl stagger
out into the darkened, shuttered street.

I used to live in a place where dogs
hunted in packs and you had to watch
all the time where you put your feet
and the houses were running with damp and the
children got asthma and bronchitis and
watched burning cars for entertainment.
In that place, loyalty was fierce and generous,
people had good parties and there was a
perverse pride that came from being
damned by poverty and prejudice.

I used to live in a place where the sea
was the undercurrent of everything.
The sea is more beautiful than anything in the world.
And grey stone dykes were the perfect expression
of a harmony of nature and culture.
And it would have been no surprise
to walk into another time,
because eternity was always promising
to break through time,
and sometimes did.
In that place,
I learned the intrinsic value of stones.

In the place where I live now,
Sumeira comes to play with painted hands,
Matthew bears five royal names of Africa
and Asoka folds fragile paper cranes.
I look out of a basement window
on trees, and many legs,
and make my way along the road,
waving to the fish-man and the pizza-man
and the girls who sell me olives.

In this place,
I love the flow of life
just waiting for the lights to change.

In all the places I lived,
there were people I loved.

I hate everything that damages people.

(KG)

Almost our first question, unspoken, is the one we ask of our
earliest carers, as we look at their faces. '*Who am I?*' If our mother,
or whoever is caring for us, smiles at us, then we know we are OK.
Of course, we do not know we are asking that question; as babies,
we are not self-aware, and will not become so for a long time yet.
We are simply trying to grasp the realities of the strange new world
into which birth has catapulted us. As our infant minds and bodies
process an extraordinary amount of data through sense-impression,
we are embarking on a lifelong journey of orientation and self-
realization.

And just as every one of us shows up, without volition, in a
specific, particular time and place, so each of us is born into
relationship. We are not born to everybody, we are born to this
woman and this man. And they, along with countless others, but,
perhaps more than any others, will shape the way we come to
answer the question, 'Who am I?' With no other initial way of
identifying ourselves, of grounding ourselves in this new world, we
rely on the clues that others give us. It is as if they are a mirror we
hold up to ourselves. 'Mirror, mirror, on the wall – am I beautiful,
am I good, am I desirable, am I lovable, am I OK?'

Nor are all or even most of the answers necessarily verbal ones. It
is well known that a small child, orphaned in time of war (say) may
be fed, kept clean and warm, receive physical care, but will still fail
to thrive deprived of holding, of soothing noises of the kind that
provide reassurance, of the gaze of affection. The effect of what is
sometimes referred to as 'unconditional positive regard', the mirroring face that says 'yes, you are loved', is a powerful one right
throughout our lives. It will give a child a basic security, a feeling of
having the right to belong in the world, the foundation for an
identity. Even if it is lacking in a parent, that unconditional positive
regard from a grandparent (often underestimated as a source of
identity) or another carer, can go a long way to compensating for
initial insecurity. The search for that kind of regard, for those who

do not receive it in childhood, is a harder road, but for many of these too the love of a partner or friend can substantially heal the damage of an impaired sense of self-worth.

The therapeutic or counselling relationship is very often a place where this damage can find healing in Western societies. And for countless men and women and children, still today, as well as in the past, Christian faith is a source of healing, as people whose experience of basic relationship has been overwhelmingly of rejection discover a profound conviction that in the eyes of Jesus they are both lovable and loved, and perhaps even, if they are fortunate, a community of people in the church who will reinforce that conviction.

Sometimes there is a tendency for those outside the church to mock the fact that apparently much of its appeal is to people who are weak, vulnerable, dysfunctional 'losers'. And while there is a real danger of emotional manipulation and abuse of power (as there is in a secular therapeutic relationship) because of the extent of the need expressed, it is a cynical cruelty to further undermine the sense of self-worth of those who are primally distressed, whose distress may well show up in damaging or self-destructive behaviour. It is an immature society and immature media which are so merciless to failure, almost universally common experience though it is.

And sometimes it is a perception and a concern of those both outside and within the church that in fact much of its dogma and practice reinforces people's sense of their own lack of self-worth, their unworthiness and corruption. Too many people have the experience, as a woman who wrote to me had, of God offered as 'punishment, fire and brimstone, in order to exclude, negate and punish those of difference'. For me, this is not the gospel. This is not the teaching or practice of the Jesus who told the story of the Prodigal Son, of the unconditional acceptance of the father. It is such a beloved story, and it is easy to understand why. It offers reconciliation and healing and new beginnings. It offers hope, and a new identity. It offers the possibility of a different kind of mirroring, one in which it is possible to take off the masks of self-defensiveness and be vulnerable; what Janet Morley describes as 'an appalled sense of self-exposure, combined with a curious but profound relief'. That sense of being acceptable, with all one's flaws and failings and secret desires known, and the liberation it brings with it, Christian faith has called grace.

But the answers we receive to the question,'Who am I?' do not just shape our most personal, individual identity. They also shape our tribal identity. We are not really accustomed to thinking of ourselves as tribal. It is a term we tend to reserve for groups of people living collectively on Pacific islands or up the uncharted reaches of the Amazon. It is an anthropological term, not applicable for modern Western societies. But we are all *anthropos*. And we all live collectively to a greater or lesser extent, so that those people who choose to live entirely in solitude, separated from other human beings, are so distinctive that one could say they qualify as members of the tribe of solitaries or hermits. And when we are asked the question, 'Who are you?', which we are asked all the time in a variety of ways, we identity ourselves in terms that are essentially tribal.

There are established, well-accepted kinds of tribal identification. The first one for most of us is probably a *family or kinship* one, and we display it in our name. For men, this is a simple matter: they identify themselves by their family of birth, and retain the same name throughout their whole lives. For most women until recently, the identification was different: it was with the family they married into, whose name they took. Today, many women choose to keep the name of their birth family when they marry. But whether they keep it or whether they change it, it is a significantly different identification from that of the vast majority of men (and its significance, I think, often underestimated), because it is a chosen one, and not simply taken as given.

Another common identification is a *national or ethnic* one, which is geographical and political and cultural, a label with many meanings. I am Scottish or French, Rumanian or Brazilian, Nigerian or Australian. For some of us, this is an easy identification to make. After my kinship one, the earliest identity that I can remember being aware of was of being Scottish. I did not know until some time later that I was also supposed to be British. I am not a political nationalist: though I support the move towards greater Scottish autonomy, I am happy for my country to remain in alliance with the other countries in the United Kingdom. But to be British is an identity which is almost devoid of content for me. I feel Scottish, it is the geography and history and culture that I belong to, that I am at home with. When I am in England, I am happy to be there, there are many, many things about it that I appreciate and admire, I acknowledge a great deal of shared history and outlook. But I am a visitor. I am not at home. I belong to the Scottish tribe.

But for me this is an uncomplicated identification. My parents and all my antecedents are Scottish. I have never, except for short periods, lived anywhere else. I live in a part of Glasgow where my grandparents were living a hundred years ago. My roots in this country go deep. I have never needed, or chosen, to uproot, to move to another country, to marry someone of a different nationality. My nationality has never been threatened; I have never been stateless, or a refugee. It is an identity I was born into, I received. As an adult, I chose to accept what I had received. For others it is not so simple.

The anthropologist from Mars

A group of about twenty-five people from a variety of backgrounds, invited to identify themselves to an anthropologist from Mars, revealed some interesting facts. Twenty-one of them identified themselves by nationality or geography. All the Scots and all the Irish who identified themselves this way did so as Scots or Irish. All the English people except one identified themselves by region or city (e.g. Cotswold, Mancunian). But then there was the African-American. And the Euro-American-Brazilian. And the person making a different kind of statement of identity who described themself as a planetary citizen.

The same group of people (and, in my own experience, most groups of people) described themselves by using other familiar tribal labels: of *gender, political leanings, religion or belief system, job or vocation,* and a few by *social class.* Within these broad categories, however, were many sub-sections:

- conservative, liberal, green, socialist, Marxist, non-political;
- Christian, Presbyterian, Methodist, evangelical, dissenter, Catholic, ecumenical, freethinker, atheist, mystic, follower of creation spirituality;
- artist, scientist, medic, researcher, student, nurse, unemployed.

Each of these constitutes its own particular tribe; furthermore, not just the grouping but a whole constellation of groupings contribute to making identity particular and distinctive. Presbyterian, for example, may have a whole different set of meanings when constellated with leftist feminist medic than when constellated with male middle-class evangelical.

Nevertheless, the categories of nationality, gender, politics, religion, job, class, are all well-used and well-known identifications. They are primary components of culture, of the collective experiences, norms and practices that shape our collective and our individual identities. They are, if you like, *building blocks of culture*. Each of them has its own habits, beliefs and ways of doing things, its own tribal customs if you like, and for a long time there has been some degree of common understanding about what constitutes each. We have thought we knew what it meant to be, for example, a Scot, or a socialist or a Catholic; what it meant to be a man or a woman, come to that. But all these categories appear to have meanings and interpretations that are changing, shifting, becoming more fluid.

What it means to be a woman, for example, has probably changed more dramatically in Britain over the past 50 years than in the previous 500, as a combination of control over fertility, political suffrage, higher education, entry in great numbers into the labour market, changes in the divorce laws, new technology, have all combined to give women a much greater degree of financial independence, and thence of personal autonomy. To be a Scot meant to be a citizen of a small country in the north of Britain whose economy was largely based on coal, steel and engineering. Now it will be to be a citizen of a country with its own Parliament responsible for all home affairs, whose economic base is technology, financial services and tourism.

Similarly, the concept of job, profession or even calling has undergone radical change. The 'job for life' is much rarer, as more and more people work on short-term contracts or are self-employed. The older industries – shipbuilding, mining, engineering, steel, where son followed father sometimes for generations into the yards or factories, down the pits or on the docks – have largely gone, their skills obsolete, their workers redundant 'Downsizing' and rationalization have left many people unemployed, or working for lower wages; the globalization of markets has both opened up new possibilities and the need for new skills, and made job insecurity endemic for people in every walk of life.

Other previously reliable building blocks of culture have also been thrown into question. Universal free education, including higher education, is looking increasingly shaky, as university fees are introduced. The social security system is changing, and many people are paying a high price for having been persuaded to opt out of employment pension schemes and enter ill-advised personal ones. Even the National Health Service, the cornerstone of the welfare state for the last 50 years, has undergone giant upheavals. Regardless of the merits or demerits of all these changes, the whole process of them has been traumatic for many. So many of the building blocks of culture seem to be not just shaky, but cracking and crumbling. The symbols of state – the law, the monarchy, the House of Lords, the police – all have taken a battering in recent years. And all of this affects our sense of identity, of who we are. As cultural unity is replaced by increasing cultural diversity, many people experience themselves as living between the cracks. Old identities shift and in many instances disappear altogether. The percentage of the population who identify themselves as Christian has reduced dramatically in the last 20 or 30 years. And the kind of community that people identify themselves with is changing too.

In the past in Britain, as in some parts of the world still today, one's community was involuntary. A person simply showed up in it by circumstance of birth, and for the most part remained in it till death. It was a community of proximity first and foremost. It was your street, your neighbourhood, your village, your town, and then by extension your country. And what street you lived in depended primarily on your social class, whether it was a miners' row of pit cottages, the tenements of the factory workers, the villas of the doctor and the lawyer or the grand town houses of the wealthy. Within that community, your identity was clear and your role was fixed; there were expectations of you, according to your family role, your social role, your occupational role. But wars, social change, new patterns of work (or non-work) and the huge increase in mobility have fragmented and sometimes destroyed these traditional communities. Now people make different kinds of collective identifications.

If we go back to the anthropologist from Mars, alongside the traditional tribal identities of work, religion and politics, we find new ones – in the mixed national identities, in the new political definitions such as 'green', 'feminist', 'earth-centred', and in the identification by cause (Amnesty International, human rights), by passion or leisure interest (sport, music, outdoor-life), or personal characteristic (drinker, joker, sleepy, enthusiast). And here are identifications which have come to be claimed as an act of courage and affirmation against cultural disapproval (gay, ex-psychiatric patient, HIV+). As we reject old identities, or they reject us, or simply disappear, our new tribes are increasingly those of shared interests, collegiality, cause and even stigma. I heard a commentator on television recently describing friendship as the new pattern of family. And as extended familes are scattered by distance and nuclear families are in the convulsions of breakdown and reformation, for many, perhaps particularly young people, this may be an accurate appraisal.

And it is not necessarily the worse for that, being, after all, quite a New Testament pattern. Jesus, who is so often held up as the ultimate nuclear family patron, against all the conventions did not form one himself, rejected his own family when they came looking for him to take him away from his unorthodox lifestyle 'for his own good' (they thought he was mad – what a familiar ring that has!) actively encouraged people to leave their parents, wives and children for his sake, and had as his closest community one that was voluntary not involuntary, and firmly rooted in friendship.

From involuntary community, we are moving more and more to voluntary identifications. Though few people, perhaps, would identify themselves as belonging to the tribe of Celtic pagan/planetary citizen/explorer/freethinker/human being, for the majority of us our identity is now a mixture of involuntary and voluntary.

When identities are secure and fixed and involuntary, the boundaries are clear. You belong within these lines. Stay within them and you will have a role, a community, a place in life. Go beyond them, however restrictive, narrow or even oppressive they may be, and you will lose all these. Not only will you lose them, but what will replace them is a great unknown. You will become an outsider, you will be alone, you will be lost. Worse, you may even become the object of revilement of those who were previously your community. Your whole identity will be threatened. When you ask, 'Who am I?', there will be no answer, or a negative one. The penalties are great. Hatred is always greatest, not for the enemy, but for the one who is felt to have betrayed his or her own. And even if there is not hatred, there are still many for whom the experience of standing against the received identity is a terrifying prospect, and then a deeply isolating experience. Anxiety, guilt, disagreement, anger, shame, low self-esteem are common feelings, whether it is for gay people coming out, for someone leaving – or joining – the church, for someone choosing not to follow the path laid out for them by family and going by another route.

In some cultures, the cost of standing out against the communal identity may be death. We are familiar with tragic stories of divided young lovers from opposite sides of a cultural conflict: Romeo and Juliet can happen as easily in Pakistan, where a couple who choose a personal identification over a collective one will be considered to have so shamed the tribe that their own family members may be the ones who kill them. A cross-community friendship in the tribal conflict that is Northern Ireland may lead to you being blown up in a pub as you discuss a wedding with your friend. But even in our own lives, a conflict over identity is also a territorial argument. It is about different maps for the same piece of ground.

As the mother of three teenagers, I am just about worn out by these conflicts because, of course, adolescence in the West is a prime time for them. Here, the search for personal identity is as strong if not stronger than the pull of collective identity, and conflicts fought over the ground of punctuality, homework, allowances and politeness are at another level both the pull of another collective identity, that of peer group, and a struggle to define oneself as having some autonomy on one's ground over against parents. When I was a teenager, I thought my parents were strict, unreasonable, insensitive and at times positively cruel. Now I see that my daughter is exactly like I was at her age (though she would loathe that thought), and I realize that my parents were remarkably long-suffering and liberal.

But I was then in the throes of challenging many of the cultural messages I was receiving when I asked, 'Who am I?', and that I attributed many of them wrongly to my parents is not their fault. Though we do not today agree about everything, I actually find I share most of their values, though I have made these a matter of choice, not unquestioning acceptance. But the greatest gift they have given me is that of 'unconditional positive regard', of love that, while it does not necessarily agree with all my choices and actions, respects my freedom to make them. This respect for persons is rooted for them in Christian faith. That is the ground from which it springs. It is quite a simple thing really. We love because God first loves us, and, how can we say we love God, whom we cannot see, if we do not love our brother or sister whom we can see (1 John 4.19–20)? It is a prodigal kind of love, but I cannot for the life of me see where there is gospel, where there is good news, if it is missing.

Of course, that kind of love is not only found among Christians. It is found everywhere in human life. And it is often not found in the church. The back catalogue of lack of love to the point of cruelty, abuse, oppression and killing which is part of the story of the church is truly appalling, and any attempt to justify it is an offence against truth. The negative, debasing and damaging messages that so many have received when they asked of the church 'Who am I?' – about their bodies, their sexuality, their role or status or occupation, their politics or religion or relationships, their very person-hood – is such a burden that it is for me, as someone who is a disciple of Jesus, a quite legitimate question whether in fact the church has added so greatly to the sum of human misery that the human race would be better off without it. I am quite often so ashamed to call myself a Christian that I think 'perhaps I'll just identify myself as a follower of Jesus. I do not find these messages in him.'

But a few things stop me doing that. The first is that I know in my heart of hearts that I have sometimes given negative messages to other people too, messages of rejection or revulsion, of irritation or contempt. Sometimes I did it without meaning to, unconscious of even doing it. Sometimes I did it knowingly, though not deliberately, it was just that 'the good that I would, I did not' (see Romans 7.19). And sometimes it was quite intentional. I try hard now not to give such messages – it matters to me not to, remembering what it feels like to have sometimes been on the receiving end of them. But I know I still do. I am a human being. I do not get terribly angst-ridden about it. I could be doing worse things, and I am not. Besides, I have long since given up any belief in my own perfection. But it does serve to remind me that just to be a member of the human race is to be compromised. Things are no better outside the church. There is cruelty, abuse, oppression and killing there too, there are a whole host of negative, debasing and damaging messages being received that owe no debt to religion.

The story of hope
But it is not just, 'Well, I'm as well here as anywhere else.' There is something more creative for me in the church. In the story of human failure that is, by and large, the story of the Christian church, another story has somehow been held, against all the odds; against

the corruption and power politics and misogyny and idolatry and self-interest, a story that generation after generation rises unconquerable, battered and bruised – yes, shouted down, sometimes to the point of near-silencing, seeming death, but always coming again to birth, the story of hope: '*They will not rob me of hope, it shall not be broken, it shall not be broken.*'

Many people have also borne witness to that story: poor people, marginalized people, excluded people mostly. They have told it not in their sermons and homilies, nor in their dogmas and doctrines, but in their flesh, in their lives. They are people who go on believing it is worth while struggling for justice, for liberation, for inclusivity, who go on planting seeds in dry land, and singing and dancing in the face of almost unbearable suffering. They go on testifying to the power, and the powerlessness, of love. They continue to give the Word flesh.

Mostly, we do not know their names. In a society obsessed with celebrity, this poem is a salutary reminder of the history not part of history.

At Garelochhead
a graveyard has been hijacked.
Who can read the names on the stones
which have been corralled
into the complex
of submarine pens, cranes
fuel stores, bunkers
and high wire fences?

These folk were buried
close to where they were born
and grew and lived and loved:
the barbed wire
has alienated them
stranded them far from home.

(Jan Sutch Pickard, from 'Treading a Path', 1995)

It is an extraordinary thing to me that the story of hope should be carried by these ordinary people without names, without power, without wealth. I mean extraordinary in the sense of awesome, and also extraordinary because they are so unsung, undervalued, unnoticed. Intentionally and explicitly, these are the people Jesus identified himself with. The authorities, the religious establishment, did not much like it then either. But because of him, and because of all the nameless people, of whom there are still a lot around, many (though not all of them by any means) in the church, I choose to identify myself with them as well as with him. Though quite often I do not feel I belong in the church, am uncomfortable in it, it is there I choose to identify with and be in solidarity with them. I have a friend who works for an aid agency, and has spent much of his life confronting the very worst things that human beings can do to each other. Asked what it was that helped him to 'keep on keeping on', he replied, 'The blood of the martyrs'. It is a rather baroque phrase, but I think these nameless ones were who he meant.

And within that somewhat uncomfortable identity, I find some things – some stories, some practices, some rituals and ceremonies, some tribal wisdom – that help me greatly in the living of my life, and particularly in the making and sustaining of relationship.

A dozen years ago, at the height of the Ethiopian famine, and during the high public profile given it in Britain by Bob Geldof and Live Aid, I remember seeing an item on the BBC television news which struck me very forcibly. It was about a young couple in the North of Scotland who had been so moved by the plight of the people of Ethiopia that they had decided to auction off all the contents of their house, and a caravan which they also owned, and give the money raised to the appeal. All their treasured possessions, lovingly collected over the years, including their wedding gifts, were given up, after they had kept only what was absolutely essential.

Of course a purist could argue that in fact they still had their jobs, their education, perhaps family resources, and they would be right. There was no sense that this couple faced destitution. Nevertheless, it was a sacrificial thing to do, and, in a British context, it was certainly an unusual thing – considered eccentric enough to make the headlines. Then, I was challenged by the sheer generosity of spirit it demonstrated. I did not think I could do that.

Now, looking back at that action, what strikes me most is not the generosity, or even questions about the wisdom of it, but the sense that that young couple must have had a profound feeling of their connectedness to the human race, a conviction of themselves as part of a body in which, if one part suffers, all the other parts suffer with it, a conviction strong enough to override their own self-interest, even what passes for common sense. For them, their well-being was tied up with the well-being of unnamed strangers on the other side of the world. They had a sense of the common good, what we in Scotland call *the common weal*, as being something in which they had an investment. They knew something of the art of sharing.

The word 'share' in English comes from the old English *scearu*, which literally means to shear or cut off. The word 'sharing' has a number of different meanings and interpretations. We use it with the meaning of 'distributing', 'apportioning', 'handing out in pieces'. This meaning has strong elements of control, of power, of reserving the right to determine who shall get a piece of the cake, and what size it shall be. My English dictionary actually uses as its example of this meaning the phrase, 'to share out food and clothing to the poor'. To me, this suggests patronage.

The second meaning for 'sharing' is 'dividing or cutting off part' of what one has, and giving it to another or others. It is to give away some, and to have less oneself. It may be understood, and often is, as a diminishing. I have vivid memories of when my children were small, trying to explain to them that cutting the cake or pie in three equal parts was the fairest way for them to eat it. Part of them, the part that had a strong sense of natural justice, could see that that was fair. But another part, the part whose eyes were bigger than its belly, could only see that it meant less for them!

The third meaning my dictionary gives for sharing (and it only gives it third) is a positive one, following the negative one and the neutral one. 'To enjoy in common with others', to participate in the use of together with others. The significant difference that I see between the first two meanings and this third one is that the former both focus on the thing which is being shared, and the latter focuses on the people it is being shared with. And between these two lines in a dictionary lies all the difference in the world.

To speak of sharing in some circles is to be branded as naïve, idealistic, out of date. At best, it is seen as a distribution strategy for the trickle-down theory, and the only question is how best to share out the crumbs from the rich man's table. More broadly, there is a fear, even among well-intentioned people, that sharing means less for us, and this at a time when not just poor people, but also the middle classes are feeling increasingly insecure. And that insecurity – about jobs, about education, about health (the kind of insecurity that much of the world has always had to live with), feeds on the fact of increasing isolation and separation from the rest of the body politic.

Baldly put, fewer and fewer people have the experience of sharing as enjoyment in common with others. We have less experience of having to rely on others, of having a pleasure enhanced by doing it with others, of seeing ourselves as a part of others, dependent upon them, and they on us, and all our politics and all our economics are exacerbating this trend. Such is the competitive nature of the market now that it gets harder and harder to engage in a demanding common task in which co-operation is both a necessity and a joy. Skills, knowledge, information are increasingly commodities to be competitively traded and jealously guarded.

In six years of living in Iona Abbey, and welcoming visitors from all over the world, but mostly from the churches in my own country, I was at first struck, and then shamed by the profound and bitter isolation in which so many people exist. I remember on numerous occasions people saying to me at the end of a week, 'This has been the best week of my life.' For those of us who lived there in community, it had probably been a run-of-the-mill kind of week, full of the mosaic of tensions, arguments, frustrations and joys of just living with others. But for people who never get close enough to others to experience real sharing, whether they live alone or with others, even the tensions were perceived as a blessing.

Because we have lost confidence in our capacity to make and sustain relationships, it is easier not to risk the attempt – and there are many substitutes now available to protect us behind our boundaries, to ensure that we need have less and less actual connection with actual people. And so we have fewer and fewer opportunities to experience common enjoyment. Even the efforts to ease loneliness can end up as two people being lonely together. In such a context, sharing is perceived not as a pleasure but as a burden. Sharing as an art, as creativity, adventure, discovery, joy, in which the sacrifice, discipline and pain that all art involves are more than compensated for by the sheer delight of creation, is very hard when you have lost confidence in your capacity to create. Breaking one's isolation open, that it may be shared and enjoyed, is a risky thing to do with so little trust in the possibility of common joy – and perhaps I mean common not just in the sense of being with others, but in the sense of joy in the small, the ordinary, the everyday.

For Christians, our Scriptures, our faith, our Lord, all teach us that blessing is first and foremost communal blessing. In the Genesis story of Jacob and Esau (Genesis 27) we are presented with a story of blessing meant to be shared as a mutual birthright, a story of abundance, sufficiency when what is provided is shared. It is a story of blessing misappropriated and abused, taken from being a communal inheritance to be a prize in a game for winners and losers.

When blessing is reduced to being a prize in a game, it becomes extremely difficult for those who wish to claim their share of the inheritance to do so outwith the rules of the game. And yet it is interesting that when these two brothers meet years later (Genesis 32 and 33), it is Esau, the one who has been cheated out of his inheritance, who is generous-spirited and forgiving, and Jacob, the cheat, who is calculating, fearful and who, immediately after their meeting, is up to his old tricks again. Jacob, having once turned his back on the art of sharing, is reduced to manipulative, premeditated striving to get what he wants. By contrast, Esau is spontaneous in expressing his feelings and faithful to his human needs. He is the teacher of the art of sharing to his brother.

My reflection on the loss of confidence in relationship is, of course, one-sided, because it is about the fears of those who feel they stand to lose. It is not about the hopes of those for whom sharing represents not just enjoyment in common with others, but a restoration of the inheritance. The catastrophically unjust world economic order requires more than just the pious hope that its winners will suddenly be persuaded to share their spoils.

But this is a question not just of economics but of faith, for those of us who seek to follow Jesus Christ. We know very well that our Lord loved poor people, hated the wrongs they suffered, and called his followers to hunger and thirst for justice. If we cannot do justice out of concern for those who live in poverty, yet we are still called to do justice for love of him. In Jesus' life and teaching, and even more in his death and resurrection, is the profound conviction that all our greeds and hungers, all our getting and spending, all our feeding of our various appetites, will not truly satisfy our deepest needs.

Nor will the idols we set up, whether they be of our own purity and blamelessness, or the pride of country, church, achievement or family. Worshipped, they will turn our stomachs, they will be bitter like the ground-down gold the Israelites in the desert were forced to drink by Moses when they had turned to the idolatry of the golden calf, and they will poison us. Only the struggle for right relationship, with others, with the earth, with the unloved parts of ourselves, ultimately with the God who is the ground of our being, can truly satisfy. Without that, it is better that we contain our emptiness, feed on the spare diet of the desert, than gorge on patriotism by killing, or protect our own children at the expense of the starvation of someone else's.

It is better to hunger and thirst for right relationships than to be filled with the wrong things. Sometimes we need to look at our emptiness, to learn from it, to discover what will really satisfy, before we are too hasty to eat what will make us sick, and deprive other people. Rich food is enticing – but it is not what satisfies day by day. There are some hungers, some thirsts, that need more substantial food. One Thursday a month in Glasgow, some people gather at noon in the city's main square to bear witness to their hunger, their emptiness, their poverty. They are not seeking money. They are looking for respect, for attentiveness, for dignity and partnership. They are resisting the low value that our society puts on them because they are poor. Their hunger is for right relationship. They welcome anyone who wants to stand beside them in that hunger.

That group of people, and others like them, challenge me again and again – what is the love that satisfies, the love which is enough, the love which is enough for everyone, not yesterday, not tomorrow, but today?

> Be thou my vision, O Lord of my heart,
> naught be all else to me, save that thou art,
> thou my best thought, by day or by night,
> waking or sleeping, thy presence my light.
>
> Riches I heed not, nor man's empty praise,
> thou mine inheritance, now and always,
> thou and thou only, the first in my heart,
> high king of heaven, my treasure thou art.
>
> (Translated from the Ancient Irish by Mary Byrne)

This ancient Irish hymn is for me a poetic expression of the need I have that there be something which relativizes all my other attachments and needs, and reminds me that I do not exist to myself alone, that I am not an island. Another image that the Christian identity has offered as a reminder is that of the Body of Christ, in which, 'if one part of the body suffers, all the other parts suffer with it, if one part is praised, all the other parts share its happiness' (1 Corinthians 12.26).

There is something profound in this most basic tenet of our faith, that we are part of one another, bound up together, one body that we struggle to discern and bear witness to. This is a struggle of spiritualities as well as a material struggle. This is a struggle between a spirituality of the market, of extrinsic worth and value addition, and a spirituality of intrinsic worth, of value for people, what I would describe as a spirituality of the gospel, no matter who holds it. It is a crucial struggle in a world in which we are always being told 'There Is No Alternative'. There are so few icons of intrinsic worth, of sharing, around at the moment, especially ones that cross the boundaries of geography and history. There are so many people struggling to break free of the rules of the game of winners and losers, who want to rediscover the art of sharing, but do not quite know how, or are held in some kind of bondage. This is a good scenario for art, for creativity, for invention.

There is an interesting little story of sharing told by Jesus in Mark 12.41–4. It is the simple story of a woman Jesus noticed while he was watching the people giving their offerings into the temple treasury. Many people gave a great deal. She, on the other hand, offered only a tiny amount. But it was all that she had. As a widow, as a poor woman, she is perhaps the most representative person in the Bible of people who are poor, marginalized, powerless, vulnerable, without status. Socially, she was one of the lowest of the low. And she is drawn in sharp contrast to the teachers of the law, who were male, powerful, and of high status, and to the rich men at the temple treasury. By the teachings of the law, she should have been able to expect care and sharing from such men. But the teachers of the law took advantage of their position to rob the widows even of their homes. And the rich men, for all that they gave a lot, gave little in comparison with her.

This story really speaks to me. Because the woman is not just a symbol. She is herself, she has her own reality, she makes herself the subject of her own life.

I see of her that she does not allow herself to be objectified or victimized by her poverty. She acts in a way that precludes all patronage, as someone making a free choice to share.

I see of her that she acts with great confidence, because she is uncalculating. The slightest calculation would have prohibited such an action. We cannot tell whether she felt the confidence she displayed, nor whether she had grounds to trust that she would be otherwise provided for. But what I see is not what she thought or felt, but what she did, her capacity for sharing of herself.

I see of her that she had a sense of value that was not dependent on her economic status. She was a woman for whom something else mattered more, something beyond herself, of which she was a part, and in which she had a part to play.

She reminds me a little of that young couple in the North of Scotland.

And for myself, in the art of sharing, in which I stumble and fall continually, I see some directions for reflection and action in this widow:

- in the struggle to move beyond the winner/loser game, which makes sharing into patronage, or worse;
- in greater boldness and confidence, greater spontaneity, less calculation not just in sharing of my substance but in sharing of myself, refusing to see that sharing as diminution, but taking the risk of discovering it to be enrichment;
- in learning to relax and enjoy and be nurtured by the value that is greater to me than my own small self, and find some of the freedom that comes from abandoning this too-great attachment.

I believe I am part of a body. But it is not just any body. It is a resurrection body. As part of that body, we carry wounds and scars. Some of them are very ugly. They are the torturer's wounds as well as the victim's. Bearing the marks is part of that belonging. But we also have to affirm and celebrate and nurture the communal joys, the life that is given back to us through the body. We share the wounds – but we also share the life. Day after day, sometimes reluctantly, sometimes angrily, sometimes with huge doubts, sometimes because there is nowhere else and no other community which will confront me so acutely with the suffering and the shame and the hope, this is the identity I choose.

...THE RESURRECTION OF THE BODY...

suffering when one part suffers
feeling the pain
not denying or suppressing
not indulging or inflicting
attending to
tending
or just bearing
till healing comes

delighting when one part delights
appreciating, applauding
giving a cheer
tingling with anticipation

shiveringly melting with enjoyment
tasting the pleasure
stretching to fill the space
curling into rest

justice in every part
joy in every part
in every part, fully alive

(KG, 1996)

5

What's It Worth?
A Question of Values

- real men don't cry
- eat up your greens for the starving children in China
- you have to have a job to be worthwhile
- you made your bed, so lie on it
- laugh and the world laughs with you, cry and you cry alone
- you get what you deserve
- feminism is a crutch for weak women
- academic qualifications are everything
- if you look good, you are good
- you have to speak properly to get on
- children should be seen and not heard
- you're too old at 30, 40, 50, 60 etc.
- if you're white, you're right, if you're black, stay back
- schooldays are the best days of your life
- time is a great healer
- heterosexuality is normative
- don't do what I do, do what I say
- it's nice to be nice
- money makes the world go round
- we are saved by being good
- a woman's place is in the home
- playing rugby is character-building
- girls aren't the right shape

- no pain, no gain
- sugar and spice and all things nice

Here is a fascinating list of cultural messages, ranging from the trivial and humorous through the poignant and painful to the bitter and downright ugly. They come in all kinds of forms, in clichés, proverbs, conventional wisdom, advertising, in the rubrics of law and religion, from the highest authorities in the land and at our mothers' knees. Most of them are readily recognizable by most of us – we have heard them often.

This a list drawn up by one group of people of cultural messages they had come to question, and for many of them, to reject. The list includes within it many of the old markers on the maps of gender, childhood, education, religion, morality and so on. For these people, the markers were misleading, or simply wrong. But in rejecting these messages, the people who made the list were also engaging in a process of re-evaluation. For every one of the statements above contains a value judgement.

Our *values*, our sense of both the absolute worth of something and its relative worth in relation to or comparison with other things, shape our choices, our priorities, our decisions about what really matters, what is most important to us. They are part of our spirituality, of what motivates us most profoundly, of what determines our ultimate concerns. And in their turn, they are shaped by the things I have been talking about in the previous chapters – by our belief systems, our sense of meaning; by our geography, our sense of place; by our history and culture, our sense of identity. And they are also shaped not just by what we receive or inherit but by what we experience and observe, by our own learning and exploration and, acutely, by crisis, that experience in which we cannot always predict how our values will show up. But because we live in a time of cultural change, when many of the things that shaped human values in previous generations are in transition, in flux, because the building blocks of culture seem to be cracking and we are trying to live between the cracks, having to make fast decisions sometimes with not a lot to fall back on, then questions of values become terribly important. Our personal values are always in an interaction with our environment, they affect and are affected by each other. Experiences such as unemployment and divorce, which have affected very large numbers of people in this country in recent years, often lead us to a deep questioning of our cultural and political and religious values, because the experiences are shaped not just by our own psychology but by the society we live in.

Culture, of course, has always changed and evolved. But the speed of change has accelerated so much this century, and the scope of life has increased hugely in a world of instant and global information and mobility. Anxiety is all around. We are asked to make value judgements thousands of times in the course of a day. Therefore, it is hardly surprising that so much of the current popular discourse is around values. And some linkages have become idiomatic.

Whose tradition?

'Traditional values', for example, is a much-quoted phrase, not least in religious circles. Now there is a provocative and even dangerous place to begin a discussion, since it immediately begs a number of questions, not least the obvious one, what is meant by it? Whose tradition, value for what, or whom?

For a large section of the media, there has been an identification of traditional moral values with the kind of Christian groups which have gained much ground in the Republican party in the USA: groups which are sometimes also known as the Religious Right, the Moral Majority. Such an identification seems to me to be extremely sloppy thinking. I find it rather lamentable that we should so easily go along with the hijacking of this terminology to a particular right-wing agenda. It is not my tradition. In fact, unless it is yours, you should be angry too at the way in which the phrase has been appropriated.

My dictionary defines 'morality' as 'principles of conduct based on a distinction between right and wrong'. In order for there to be a tradition there has to be some degree of consensus in a society as to what it believes to be right and what it believes to be wrong. I, for example, am a Scot. In my society, I think there is a fairly high degree of consensus, which has held for many generations, that freedom of conscience is right and coercion is wrong, that equality for all persons is right and inequality is wrong, that free and universal education, and the access to it, is right and the denial of that is wrong, that assuming responsibility for the care of the poor and vulnerable in our communities is right and that abnegating or devaluing that responsibility is wrong, that justice is right and injustice is wrong, that integrity, indivisible between public and private life, is right and disintegration is wrong.

This is not to say that these values have always been practised – far from it. You could not be a woman, or a poor person, or an Irish Catholic in Scotland and claim that. Nor does it mean that there are not plenty of voices dissenting from these values.

But that these principles of right and wrong have enough support to constitute a tradition is evident in practice. The history, culture and politics of Scotland give ample evidence of this tradition – from land struggles to the Disruption in the Church of Scotland of the nineteenth century which took place over a question of freedom from patronage; from a strong labour movement to the commitment to state education; from a continually expressed willingness to pay higher taxes in order to support better public services, to, in more recent years, the deep resentment of the poll tax of the early 1990s. Politically this tradition is enshrined in the principle of the sovereignty of the people over the sovereignty of Parliament.

These are my traditional moral values. You could say that these are principles of modernity, of the Enlightenment, democratic, rational and humanitarian. They are the ones I was raised with in home, school and university and in the politics and civic society of my country. I have a passionate attachment to them. I think they have a part to play in Scotland, in the United Kingdom and as we participate in Europe and the rest of the world.

But they are also, unquestionably, and for me primarily, values of my Christian tradition, of my church. When I reflect with some ambivalence as I frequently do, on my Presbyterian identity, and contemplate the possibility of whether l would feel more at home as a Quaker or an Episcopalian, which in many respects I think I would, there is a pull, a connection to something so strong in me that it is as if it were in my bones. All my life I have been nurtured in the conviction of *the priesthood of all believers*, not just as a theory but as a practice. In civic terms, this translates into a commitment to democratic values. As a Scottish Presbyterian, with a church history of egalitarianism, freedom of conscience and a high regard for education, it would be hard for me to be non-democratic. As a citizen, I am unable to expect less of the church than I do of a democratic state.

The relationship between church and state in Scotland has been a dialectic one over hundreds of years; sometimes fraught and full of conflict, but with much less of the separation of spheres seen in other countries, and, I think with an acceptance of the legitimacy of the church having the right and perhaps even the duty to express its opinions on questions of society, state and governance (though, of course, the right to impose these opinions is quite another matter). Because it was a dynamic relationship, the Enlightenment in Scotland was in part shaped by the church, and in turn shaped the Church of Scotland today. And in recent years, this relationship has become increasingly ecumenical. It does not surprise Scots today to see industrial chaplains mediating in disputes, or bishops highlighting social justice concerns of poverty and homelessness. Representatives of the churches were full participants in the Scottish Constitutional Convention, which did important work towards securing a Scottish parliament. Indeed, its chairman was a churchman. This kind of involvement has never caused the kind of furore seen elsewhere – perhaps because there is not the same constitutional confusion over establishment.

For me, this democratic tradition in both church and state is a core value. It is the passion and logic underlying a commitment to feminist and popular theology and liturgy in the church, and a commitment to a participative democracy that enables women and poor people to be fully involved in political decision-making. In both of these commitments, I am simply endeavouring to take both my religious tradition and my political tradition at their word: that the priesthood of all believers actually means all; that democracy is not just for a male, bourgeois, political class.

So it is a source of some fascination to me that what for me are traditional Christian values, rooted in my church history, are the very same ones that would be considered by others to be the secular, anti-Christian values they are so fearful of. Different maps, I guess.

However, we live in a multicultural, multi-faith democracy. Therefore I also believe that other traditional moral values must be represented and heard, and I expect to, and do, learn from these other traditions constantly. Because, out of my traditional values, I believe in freedom of conscience, I can do no less. Being heard, they must then take their chances. And of course there is a huge area of overlap, perhaps more than we often admit to, between the value systems of different traditions.

We still live in a society where there are a number of commonly held beliefs about what is right and what is wrong (though perhaps less of these than in times past) and they are the basis for the rule of law. There is still a consensus, broadly drawn from the Ten Commandments, but finding its corollaries in the teachings of other faiths and belief systems, that it is wrong to steal what does not belong to you, to use physical violence against others, to borrow without repaying your debts. From this distinction between what is right and what is wrong, we make judgements about who is in the right or wrong, and we condemn and punish accordingly. We agree that this kind of distinction and discernment is neccessary in order to preserve individual rights, protect the weak and maintain the common good. This we do in our codes of law.

Except that as soon as we make this kind of statement, we immediately begin to qualify it. 'It's wrong to kill, except when ...' 'It's wrong to steal, unless ...' 'It's wrong to default on your debts, but ...' (fill in the blanks according to contemporary practice). Furthermore, we also begin to ask questions about these qualifications, especially when they are enshrined in law. Who decides what are to be the exceptions to the rules – and in whose interest? The intense debate about sleaze and corruption among politicians is inevitable and necessary; since they are the people more than anyone else whom we mandate to make these decisions on our behalf when they legislate, we want to be assured that they will practise what they preach, or not preach at all.

But unless an entirely pure following of, say, the Ten Commandments, is to be adopted (which would have huge consequences of the kind that are visible in countries that adopt a religious code for political governance) we have to interpret, not just what right and wrong consist of but what they consist of in any given situation. It is no use populist politicians and tabloid newspapers sounding off about the evils of relative morality. It is implicit in the very notion of the rule of law itself. Clearly, right and wrong are not so simple as they first sound.

And at a time when the consensus about the interpretation of morality is fragmenting in many areas (or at least, since the power to impose uniformity of morality has weakened in the face of a more pluralist society, with democratic freedoms and a wider range of information and possibilities on which to base choices) it may be tempting to look to the churches to provide simple answers to complex moral questions. Certainly, that is what many in the churches live in hope of.

Furthermore, even if the consensus about what constitutes right and wrong is undergoing a lot of reinterpretation, in everything from genetics to sexuality to the nature of work, there is also a consensus about what constitutes happiness or well-being, and this may be somewhat stronger. Though it may not be codified in law, it is certainly maintained by our economics, sustained by our practice and reflected in our media. The consensus is that it is better to be rich (or at least comfortably off) than poor, better to be full than empty, better to have occasion to laugh than occasion to cry. Few of us would consider ourselves blessed, never mind being well, if we were poor, hungry and sad.

Radical re-evaluation

The big difficulty about Jesus as an arbiter of moral values, of right and wrong, or indeed of aesthetic or hedonistic values (the values of beauty and pleasure) is that throughout his life, teaching, ministry, death and resurrection as told to us in the Gospels, he engages in a fierce re-evaluation of all that we consider to be right, good and just. A curse upon your good name, he says; do good to those who hate you, he says; if anyone hits you once, let him do it again, he says; invite the thief to take more, he says; don't judge, he says, don't condemn, he says, love your enemies, he says. These verses from Luke's Gospel (see 6.27–37) drive a coach and horses through any notion of principles based on right and wrong, and the distinction thereof. Either they subvert the principles, or they depart from them entirely.

Imagine the implications, imagine the consequences if we took Jesus at his word. But more than that, this is so offensive to any sense of natural justice. For God 'is good to the ungrateful and the wicked'. Sometimes I wonder that we do not find it more offensive, this passage. Are we so familiar with it that it has ceased to shock us? Or has it been so pietized that it has simply ceased to have any meaning for us? Taken as a morality for a church, an ethic for a society, what would it mean? That we did not lock up criminals, that we did away with the police, with the army? This sounds quite unworkable. Do we conclude that Jesus did not actually mean what he said? Or that he was a dangerous lunatic? If anyone suggested this as a present-day ethic for penal practice or immigration policy, they would be in grave danger of being deported!

72

But perhaps these are not supposed to be a guideline for a society. It has often been assumed that what Jesus was offering was an individual spiritual ethic, a new personal morality, appropriate for individual relationships. Still, it is hard to see how that makes it any easier or less offensive. I could, for example, be opposed to the restoration of capital punishment, think it is wrong to hit children, and find myself in profound agreement with an ethic opposed to the use of any kind of physical coercion. On the other hand, could such an ethic be used to support a situation in which wives are expected to tolerate being used by brutal and controlling husbands as a punch-bag. I am outraged and offended by the notion that the appropriate response to domestic violence is to go on letting it happen, to forgive and endure. Too many women and children, and men too, have been physically and spiritually maimed, even murdered, by that kind of thinking. At what point does a personal morality become a political one? One battered woman may be personal, domestic. What about two, ten, a hundred, a thousand? What's the cut-off point between a personal tragedy and a social disease?

And is it possible to deplore killing as a personal act, but condone it when it is done in the name of the state? Do we not become rather dangerous people, alienated from ourselves, too like the corrupt politicians we abhor, in fact, if we have one set of practices in private and another in public?

Or take stealing, I can see a degree of natural justice in the poor stealing from the rich and, though I would not condone lawbreaking of this kind, I might be inclined to consider extenuating circumstances. I would, in fact, exercise judgement. Furthermore, since I like to think of myself as not in thrall to material possessions, and try to sit quite lightly to the ones I have, it is not beyond the bounds of possibility that if I caught someone trying to make off with my television, I might offer him my video-recorder also. But what if someone takes my legs with a car trying to save ninety seconds at a pedestrian crossing? Should I offer my arms too? Where does it stop being personal and become political? Is one Maxwell pensioner robbed of a peaceful old age personal or political? Is twenty, or two hundred?

Is God good to Rosemary West? This God who is good to the wicked and ungrateful?

The morality and ethics of the Gospels can become a corner into which we paint ourselves from which there is no way out. It is common to hear preachers say that the Sermon on the Mount is an ideal. Is that really the only realistic point of view for Christians when passages like this one from Luke, and many others like it seem to suggest that we are supposed to depart not just from bad morality but from good? In this corner, it does not really make much difference whether your morality is a liberal one or a conservative one. Everyone's notions of justice, of right and wrong, are offended in this corner. Not only is it immoral, it is politically even-handed.

Because there is no getting away from the fact that this sermon of Jesus demonstrates very starkly what is the ground bass, the bottom line of the gospel. It is reiterated too many times to be accidental, or a redaction, or a political interjection – in the stories of the Prodigal Son, of the Labourers in the Vineyard, in the parables of the Kingdom, in the anointing stories. It is reiterated in the crucifixion. The bottom line of the gospel, the good news, is not good morality, but gratuity, grace, that which is utterly undeserved.

It does make one wonder whether those who call for a Bible-based morality have actually read the Bible. To take morality, the principles of right and wrong, as the basis of Christianity, is to stumble on the starting line. It would be better to say that Christianity starts when morality stumbles. That is not to say that there is not great ethical teaching in the Scriptures, or that there is no morality in Christian faith. But the two cannot be equated. This may be labouring a point. But if we take morality, if we take principles of right and wrong, as the basis, the foundation stone, the core value of Christianity, we are lost. We will never get out of the corner. Let us try another starting point. Let us try family values.

The inclusive family

'Family values' is another term which has come to have a somewhat loaded meaning. It has become very much associated with a particular agenda pertaining to the nuclear family, hostile to divorce, alternative patterns of family and homosexuality. It is a term which, according to how we feel about these things, evokes either enthusiasm or deep suspicion.

Unfortunately, neither the Bible nor the history of the church is unambiguous in this respect. The great heroes and patriarchs of the Old Testament might not be considered the best role models for the youth of today, practising as they did a range of behaviour (from adultery and concubinage through surrogacy and procurement to rape and incest) that would shock the *Sun*.

And even in the New Testament, family values do not seem to mean precisely what we might imagine. Jesus, more than anyone else, relativized the family, pointed out its idolatrous potential and made the bonds of the Spirit, of love and grace, more binding than those of blood or law.

Along with the punishment of those who do wrong, our society expects those who do right to be rewarded. And the ethic of our society is one of success. But Jesus subverted morality, the whole notion of right and wrong, by suggesting that the love of God extended to the failed and the ungrateful and the wicked, was in fact unconditional, and that the way to be part of the family of God was to love even one's enemies. Furthermore, he suggested that the most disabled people in this subversive view of the world were the ones who were most convinced of their own righteousness.

We see something of this subversive kind of judgement in the writings of the prophet Ezekiel. It is found not just in the gathering in and tending of the lost, the weak, the sick and the hurt which are the marks of the good shepherd. It is also found in the uncompromising judgement on those who 'are not satisfied with eating the best grass, but trample down what they don't eat, who drink the clear water and muddy what they don't drink, while the other sheep go hungry and thirsty' (see Ezekiel 34.18–19).

And this re-evaluation finds crystal-clear expression in the famous passage on the judgement on the nations in Matthew 25. It is entirely free of any notion of deserving or undeserving; it does not say 'Receive the stranger in your homes, unless he's an illegal immigrant'; it does not say 'Only visit the prisoners of conscience'; it just says, 'When you did it for the least important, the most marginalized, the most redundant to the market, you did it for me' (see Matthew 25.45). Above all, it is uncalculating.

The way above all in which Jesus encouraged his followers to think of their relationship to God was as father. Now in spite of all the problems this presents to people today – the reinforcing of patriarchy, the neglect of the feminine, bad or absent models of fathering and so on – all of which are real, and require to be engaged with – we should not let this divert us from the fact that Jesus invited people to enter a relationship with God which was intimate, familial and, above all, loving.

We are all familiar by now, whether from popular psychology, because we have experienced it, or because we have felt its lack, with the characteristics of good parenting. It should be nurturing, offering us safety and security to grow with confidence. It should be encouraging. It should be firm, setting clear boundaries, and yet fair, allowing us as we mature to assume reponsibility for our own boundaries. But above all, it should be characterized by unconditional love (a different thing, of course, from unconditional approval), that is to say, the conviction that we are loved for ourselves, and not according to how beautiful, successful, talented or well-behaved we are. To borrow a metaphor from economics, in good parenting, market forces do not apply. To good parents, we have intrinsic value, just by virtue of our being. Their love is not dependent on extrinsic value addition, and does not vary according to our desirability or lack of it to others. They give us their love free. It is gratuitous. It is grace.

Even in dysfunctional families, this free love operates. Single parents display it. The mothers of drug addicts demonstrate it, as they sit beside the beds of people whom everyone else has discarded as beyond rescue, as they shed bitter tears. The fathers of unemployed, unskilled, unattractive teenagers embody it, in their anger and frustration for lives that are offered so little opportunity. Not always, but remarkably often. In fact, one could make a very good case for the proposition that they demonstrate it to an extraordinarily high degree, because they do it in such very difficult, even hostile circumstances, with very little external support or resource, and because they get so little payback from their offspring in the form of achievement, success or at least good behaviour. What grace, to go on loving under these conditions. Could Jesus possibly be referring to them as blessed, happy? Because, of course, the gratuity is only free to the children. The cost to the parents is very high.

It is my understanding of Christian faith that it was into such a familial relationship with God that Jesus invited his followers. We who are Christians are invited to trust the fact that we have intrinsic worth in the eyes of God. We are family, made in the image of God. And because we are loved, we can be forgiven, healed, contained, set free, we can grow. To know our intrinsic worth to God, that in spite of all we do we are of infinite value, is to be saved.

But if we are family, we are not alone, It is not just me, God and Jesus in a cosy threesome. I am not the only loved one. To be born into the family of God is to be born into a new relationship with all who are made in the image of God. Grace is not just mine. Who is my brother? Who is my sister? These relationships go far beyond blood, kinship, nationality, race, religion, politics. If I would call God my father, then Saddam Hussein is my brother, the woman-hater is my brother, the woman who takes my husband is my sister. Of course, I do not control how they understand their relationship with me. That is not my responsibility. Mine is to live in relationship as I understand it. And Jesus said, 'Do for others just what you want them to do for you' (Luke 6.31).

When family values are extended beyond our front door, or beyond our church walls, or beyond our national borders, questions of morality take on a somewhat different perspective. It is not that right ceases to be right, or wrong ceases to be wrong, it is more that we cease to be so innocent. These are also family values, about which Jesus says that, the measure you use for others is the measure God will use for you. By the family values of the Gospels, the International Monetary Fund, for example, with its Structural Readjustment Programme for poor country debt, looks like the worst kind of loan shark.

But by that measure, it is not just the IMF. We are all a little tarnished. We are all under judgement. In the family values of the gospel, morality is viewed through the eyes of love, not love through the eyes of morality. Perhaps another way of saying that is that though someone or some group may have offended us, hurt us, acted towards us with hostility, even though we are absolutely opposed to their actions, still we do not exclude them from the family.

Of course, the decision to love our enemies does not therefore mean that we can dispense with morality. Rather the reverse, in fact. It immediately confronts us with the question, what is the good thing, the right thing, to do in this situation, if inclusion rather than exclusion is our starting point. Morality does not disappear. It is just that its starting point is different. I fear there is no escape from difficult questions. With a family value of intrinsic worth, how do we engage with a market value of extrinsic worth and not become dangerously disintegrated? With a family value of gratuity, of generosity, of extravagance even, how do we engage with a political value of mean-spiritedness? With a family value of personhood, how do we engage with a cultural value of depersonalization? With a family value of care, where is justice? Moral questions, every one.

For me, it helps to start small, I seek to recover the ability to imagine the other as person – not as enemy, not as statistic, not as problem, not as promising material for evangelism, but as person, the way I want to be seen as person: in relationship. Christianity is about the triumph of grace over law. As the old theological language would have it, we are justified by faith, not by works. In this understanding of Christianity, faith is not intellectual assent to a set of propositions, neither is it a morality of right or wrong, or even a beautiful ethic. It is a relationship with Jesus Christ, through whom we are invited to be righteous, that is, in right relationship with God, with other people, with ourselves. And this right relationship is not attained by being right or wrong, good or bad. We are all flawed people; in the old language, we are all sinners. The relationship is received, not achieved. In the memorable paraphrase of one Will Campbell, 'we're all bastards, but God loves us'.

In fact, one can make a very good case for Jesus as being someone who continually subverted the traditional moral values of his society, the principles of what was right and what was wrong. Traditional moral values about the place of women, the role of the family, attitudes towards money and possessions, the nature of servanthood, the priority of the poor and dispossessed in God's economy were all challenged in the re-evaluation of what it meant to be a human being in right relationship.

So although I have a deep attachment to what I consider to be my traditional moral values, they are relativized for me by this primary loyalty to another relationship which takes precedence over any other agenda, political or religious. If the nature of that relationship I find best expressed and summed-up in the gospel story, and believing as I do that personal and political relationship are integral, that I cannot be one person in private and another in public, that I cannot privatize my faith, then of course that challenges all my practice, and I must bring that to bear on my political engagement. What, for example, does the unconditional love, forgiveness and generosity of the father of the Prodigal imply if applied to penal policy? What to parenting, marital breakdown? What is the challenge it presents to the morally correct elder brother part of us and of our society?

And if I believe in a relationship that unconditionally values every person regardless of status, wealth, success or virtue, that bestows intrinsic worth on the worst as well as the best, with no value addition necessary, how am I to regard an economic system, and its underlying spirituality, which determines worth purely by external market forces, which actually relieves poor people, disabled people, unemployed people, single parents, elderly people, of their intrinsic worth?

We take care of what we value. Ultimately, people know whether and how they are valued by their society, and by its political institutions. Who do we give value to? Because Jesus, declaring judgement on the nations, said, 'Whenever you did this for one of the least important of these brothers and sisters of mine, you did it for me' (Matthew 25.40). I cannot see that this question is any less crucial now than it has ever been.

Spending power

Our society has undergone a huge shift, accelerated in recent years, from defining our work (in particular, but other aspects of life too) in terms of cultural value to defining it in terms of economic value. 'Everything has its price.' It is often quoted, and we have had to learn to put a price on our skills, our experience, our time: to market ourselves. Values are about deciding what is most important to us, about the worth of things, and about setting priorities.

If we take a sheet of paper, draw two circles on it, one titled Money and the other called Time, we are looking at the two currencies that people use most in our society. These are what we spend, time and money, and we are more and more accustomed to having to translate our spending of time into the currency of money. 'Time is money' we say, and we calculate our earnings by time. If we then make of these circles pie charts, slicing them up according to how we spend our money (a certain percentage for housing, for taxation, for insurance and so on) and how we spend our time (a certain percentage for sleep, for work, for time with our children, our friends and so on), we can get a real insight into what our core values really are, into what really matters to us, rather than what we think, say or hope they are. Above all, our values show up in what we do. It is where we put our theories into practice, practise what we preach – a fact which is well known to pollsters and predicters confounded by the results of elections.

For most of us, there is a fixed component in this spending. We have to live somewhere – but our values will show up in what kind of house we choose, whether we live in the country, the suburbs or in the middle of the city. We work to support our children – but there is an underlying value that having children is something so important to us that we give up other kinds of spending to support it. One person may choose to spend a lot of money on a car because the freedom it allows is a high value for them, another may choose not to have a car because ecological concern is a higher value than personal mobility. Our constraints are often the result of previous value choices and judgements.

And in the much smaller area of spending power which is not fixed, what is left over when the basics are accounted for, our values may show up very clearly. We may think we have a high value for our children or our friends, but we may spend only five minutes of the day actually being with them. And a time chart from which solitude is entirely absent may suggest someone who is uncomfortable being alone, who does not place much value on their own company.

Our value choices affect other people too, not just us. Every day we make moral choices, ethical decisions without ever noticing that we are making them, because they are based on value judgements that are so much part of who we are that they have become wholly unconscious. In every trip to the supermarket we are participating in an attribution of value one way or another. When people are terribly hurt or confused at being accused of making, for example, racist or sexist statements when they had no intention of hurting anyone's feelings, they are mostly acting out of quite unconscious and unexamined value judgements which, when examined, they would find were not actually the values they want to display. Racism and sexism awareness education is not at all intended to make us feel guilty or like nasty people: it is simply to help us to bring these unconscious value judgements into a place where they can be looked at, and help us to ensure that our actions are consistent with our intentions, that we do what we say we want to do.

In the Forum Theatre methods developed by the Brazilian director August Boal, there is one exercise called 'spectacting'. In it, people are divided into two groups. One group is then given a scenario to role-play, to act out. The other group watches the scenario unfold, without comment, till the story ends. Then the group starts acting out the scenario again. But this time, any member of the onlooking group who thinks the role-play should be different, who does not agree with a particular interpretation, can stop the action by saying 'Stop', can replace one of the characters and, if they choose, alter the course of the action, bring a new perspective, a fresh direction. If no one chooses to engage in this way, the scenario runs on to its original conclusion. This is a wonderfully clear way to illustrate the point that, without action, without engagement, without the investment of our time and energy, nothing changes, no matter how passionately we feel or how strong our convictions. We can revalue people, situations, places, only through what we do.

But the problem about all of this when we are looking at our deepest values, at what really matters to us, is that so much of it, certainly in the church, seems so ineffably dull. Just to say the word 'worthy' is to sound dull, uninspiring.

There is a story about the Pre-Raphaelite poet, Dante Gabriel Rossetti. Referring to his sister, Christina Rossetti, also a poet, and a devoted Christian, he said in a way that possibly only a brother could, 'If Christina's heart is like a singing-bird, why does she dress like a pew-opener?' Pew-opener, presumably, being a Victorian synonym for all that was dowdy, dreary and dull.

A frivolous remark, perhaps, and yet one which rather tellingly illustrates a huge public perception, now as then, of what being a Christian is all about – dutiful and worthy at best, and at worst boring, correct, uninspiring and deeply unattractive. It sounds like the kind of thing laddish magazines say about feminists – the ultimate put-down. As the Puritan poet John Milton discovered in *Paradise Lost*, it is easier to make the bad enticing than the good; fallen women and errant sons somehow seem to touch public sympathy far more than dutiful elder brothers and Martha banging on about the housework. Even Jesus seemed more drawn to the company of the out-and-out sinners. Money, sex, power may not have the same worth, but they often seem much more attractive; they are the currency of desire. And who of us can, in our heart of hearts, say that our desire is valueless to us?

In part, Christians only have ourselves to blame. We have been so often so devoted to turning Christian faith from being a life-giving relationship into being a system of bourgeois morality, in which respectability is the highest value, that we have drawn a very clear dividing line between the righteous and the prostitutes and sinners and put ourselves on the righteous side. Of course, it is the more comfortable side. Unfortunately, it is not the side that Jesus is on; and in the final analysis, it is not the church, and even less we Christians that are the real attraction to so many. It is Jesus who compels. This translation by Rowan Williams is from the Welsh poetry of the early nineteenth-century farmer's wife, Ann Griffiths.

> Under the dark trees, there he stands,
> there he stands; shall he not draw my eyes?
> I thought I knew a little
> how he compels, beyond all things, but now
> he stands there in the shadows. It will be
> Oh, such a daybreak, such bright morning,
> when I shall wake to see him
> as he is.
>
> He is called Rose of Sharon, for his skin
> is clear, his skin is flushed with blood,
> his body lovely and exact; how he compels
> beyond ten thousand rivals.
>
> ('I Saw Him Standing', translation 1994)

Now this is the kind of poem, baroque and extravagant, carnal, erotic even, that can get people shifting uncomfortably in their seats and looking embarrassed. It is so passionate, so extreme. Or how about this from George MacLeod, to be a little more Presbyterian, a little more masculine:

> His life from start to finish was like a sun giving warmth to all who came within its rays; but in his cross that same sun became focused, as through a lens, till the warmth of his example becomes so concentrated as to set on fire all that it touches. That resolute persistency, that doing battle with the hilt when his sword was gone ... attracts people, draws them, thrills them. You cannot say why; it is just that it does.
>
> (*Govan Calling*, 1934)

Jesus does not compel so much because of his goodness or his worthiness. He compels because of his love. Perhaps something of the compelling power that love possesses was demonstrated in the extraordinary outpouring of feeling surrounding the death of

Princess Diana. Those who complain that she was privileged, that she did no more good works than many more unsung, seem to me to be missing the point. The response of so many was not at all because she was good, but because she loved, was needy, was wounded and loved – doing battle with the hilt when the sword was gone. It has such attraction. It is a different kind of spending power.

The power of Jesus to attract has led countless numbers of every background and culture, of every age and description for two thousand years, to follow when he called. Men and women have sacrificed everything, including their lives, and counted it well lost. 'Leave home or brothers or sisters or mother or father or children or fields for me and for the gospel' said Jesus (see Mark 10.29), and they did. Or at least, some of them did. There is a story in the Gospels of a rich young man, drawn to Jesus, the 'Good Teacher'. I expect it was the highest compliment he could bestow, to be good. All his life had been dedicated to being good. But, 'Why do you call me good?' says Jesus. 'Only God is good.' Maybe the rich young man thought being good would be enough. But not for Jesus. 'Give up everything you have, and come and follow me.' Love me more than anything else, more than your goodness, more than your wealth. But it was too hard for the young man. He went away, sad, because he was very rich. Even Jesus could not draw him to go beyond his own self-interest. The love of money is a powerful value.

At this time, the Jubilee 2000 petition of churches and aid agencies, aware of the vast preventable human suffering caused by global debt, is urging the West to cancel much of the poorest countries' debt burden, drawing on the biblical notion of jubilee at the millennium. In the Old Testament, the prophet Amos spoke passionate words to a people of great prosperity, notable religious piety and apparent security. Good people, seemingly, righteous even. But Amos saw that prosperity was limited to the wealthy, that it fed on injustice and oppression of the poor. Religious observance was insincere, and security more apparent than real. His was a text of judgement, not on the prostitutes and sinners, but on those that oppress the poor, twist justice and cheat people out of their rights. 'You people hate anyone who challenges injustice,' cried Amos (Amos 5.10). But the God of justice, who is on the side of the poor, was angry. 'He will sweep down like fire, and no one will be able to put it out,' cried Amos (5.6).

Love is not concerned
with whom you pray
or where you slept
the night you ran away
from home
love is concerned
that the beating of your heart
should kill no one.
(Alice Walker, 'Love Is Not Concerned', 1984)

Amos, like all the prophets of the Old Testament, leaves us in no doubt that whether the beating of our hearts kills anyone is a big issue for God. We know that the crisis of global debt kills people. Debt repayments (in amounts vastly more huge than those originally borrowed, which were actually repaid long ago) are diverting resources from even the most basic health provision, from education, from infrastructure. Land that used to grow food for people is now used to grow cash crops to generate income to service debt repayment. The conditions laid down by the International Monetary Fund and the World Bank in exchange for debt rescheduling (basically, giving people a little more time to pay) would cause uproar if they were applied in Western countries, such is their harshness. All this is well known. It is a situation of profound injustice. It is killing people to repay interest to the West. And as long as we accept this, do not resist it, then the beating of our hearts is killing someone.

I am complicit in this. My hands are not clean. But no amount of exhortation to duty can make me do things differently. We are not moved by lectures, or preachers telling us what we ought to do. They fall into the category of worthy but boring, correct but deeply unattractive. What moves us is passion: love and courage, compassion and kindness, humour and wonder and delight. And also anger. Probably it is better to be moved by anger at injustice than not to be moved at all. Jesus was certainly moved by anger on a number of occasions. But anger alone is a dangerous passion. It can eat us up, make us damagingly self- and other-destructive, narrow and fanatical and self-righteous. And if we have only anger, then others cease to be people, subjects of their own lives, and become instead types, categories – victims, causes, statistics. To see the peoples of Africa and Latin America in this way would be to compound the injustice. They are not to be defined by the wrongs inflicted on them by others. It is not enough to hate injustice. We have to have an accompanying love.

The real question for me is the same one that Jesus asked of the rich young man. Do I love Jesus enough to follow him? Does he compel, does he attract, does he draw us to love him more than anything else: family, home, wealth, comfort, security? Can I be saved from my complicity with injustice? What really moves me? Does it move me enough to get up and walk, to get up and walk on the water, to get up and go out and do something?

The love that moves is always a personal one, experienced personally. And because we are different, we experience it in different ways – or perhaps it would be more accurate to say that we are led into it in different ways. Some of us will be drawn by a love of justice, some by a love of this beautiful planet, in all its tragedy and potential. Some of us will love children especially, our own and others'. Some of us will see Jesus in the face of our lover, or in the faces of the people who pass us on the street. Our love as persons may be for one person or for many, for one place or for all. Whatever way we find it, the love that moves, that compels, is the love that opens our hearts to the whole. It is not the love that narrows, seeks to possess, to control, to bind. It is the love that widens, releases, sets free, takes delight. It is sacramental, both a sign and a symbol of wholeness. It is the love that takes us beyond ourselves, beyond our own self-interest, makes us capable even of self-sacrifice. When we participate in that love, it is my faith that we are being drawn into the love of Christ.

Others in our trinitarian faith describe the divine love that moves us in different ways. Here is Sean McDonagh, the Irish Columban missionary priest and ecologist, finding the One in the many:

> The Holy Spirit is the source of all unity. All attraction, all bonding, all intimacy and communion flows from the Spirit. Each of these relationships is sacred to the Spirit, who inspires all fruitfulness and creativity, the signs of true bonding and intimacy. From the Spirit comes the great urge to heal what is broken, re-unite what is separated and recreate the face of the earth.
>
> (*To Care for The Earth*, 1986)

Or Thomas Merton, finding the many in the One: 'There is a conversion of the deep will to God that cannot be effected in words – barely in a gesture or ceremony. There is a conversion of the deep will and a gift of my substance that is too mysterious for liturgy, and too private' (*The Sign of Jonas*, 1976).

Always we are coming back to the language of the lover and the beloved; always there is the attraction, the desire, the surrender, the abandonment, the totality of which relativizes all our other attachments and sets us free to love. Always the paradox that only in the given life is the truly given-back life: 'Anyone who leaves home for me and for the gospel will receive much more, a hundred times more, and persecutions as well; and in the age to come, eternal life' (see Mark 10.29–30). What we give away shall return completed. To find your life, you must first lose it. Love is concerned that the beating of your heart should kill no one.

It is extremely scary, that kind of self-surrender. Who do we, in our self-possessed, autonomous culture, trust enough to give ourselves in that way to? Who do we want to judge the thoughts and desires of our hearts? We are, after all, not so good. We may do all the right kind of praying. We may never sleep with the wrong people. But we cannot guarantee that the beating of our hearts kills no one. With whom dare we be exposed, laid open? Not with one who cannot feel sympathy for our weaknesses. Jesus encouraged his followers to have confidence, to approach God; because that is where we are being led, into the presence of God, which is grace.

The rich young man was challenged to conversion, to re-evaluation, a transforming of his scale of values. It was too much for him – he thought he had too much to lose. And yet, we are told, he went away sad. Perhaps he came to feel he had really lost much more. Perhaps he changed his mind. Still, for the sake of the world which is precious, which, we read, God loved so much, we are being challenged to re-evaluate, to tip the values of the market upside down.

> This could be our revolution:
> to love what is plentiful
> as much as
> what's scarce.
> (Alice Walker, from 'We Alone', 1984)

We take care of what we value. If we do not take care of it to the best of our ability, it means that whatever we profess, we do not really value it. As people of faith, our conviction of the intrinsic worth of the creation flows from our conviction about the value of the Creator, about the goodness of God. The creation is an expression of the creative love of God, who has created it, revalued it and sustains it. As part of that creation, we know ourselves also to be valuable and valued – not perfect, not flawless, but precious and loved as we are. Intrinsic worth, the interconnectedness of all things, the miracle of the ordinary are not just about the value of other people, other species, other forms – they are about our value. These convictions affirm us in our life and aspirations; they make demands and require sacrifice of us, but they are also hope and promise and delight.

6

To Love and to Cherish?
A Question of Care

After returning from acting as an official monitor in the first free elections in Malawi for many years, a friend spoke, obviously moved, of seeing women with small children, carrying babies on their backs, walking many miles to their nearest polling station; of elderly people standing in long queues in the fierce heat for many hours; of people going to extraordinary lengths to exercise the right to vote, scenes reduplicated many times over in South Africa. She returned into the middle of the European elections in Britain, with their low polls and widespread lack of interest. More locally, there are councillors elected in parts of Glasgow on turnouts of just over 10 per cent. *We take care of what we value.* What bonds of care have been broken that significant numbers of people in this country find this democratic right, a fundamental one, which many people in this country gave their lives to attain, to have so little value for them?

Every day in this country, hundreds, perhaps thousands of women, of children, of vulnerable old people, of people with mental and physical disability, are subjected to extreme abuse extending to life-threatening physical violence, by the people from whom they should most be able to expect love and respect. *We take care of what we value.* What bonds of care have been broken, and what bonds have become shackles, for people to value so little, to degrade so much, their environment, their families, themselves?

I know a woman who for three years lived with her family in an empty rat-infested tenement building on the south side of Glasgow rather than accept one of the sub-standard houses she was offered by the Housing Department. For three years she did battle with the biggest bureaucracy in Europe, for three years she cared for a family which included a sick husband and a disabled child in a house with no services. For three years she and her family crossed the river first thing in the morning and last thing at night to use the nearest public toilets. After two years, under extreme official pressure, tired, dispirited and fearful, she accepted the offer of one of these houses. She lay awake all night. The next morning, she went back to the Housing Department to tell them she was refusing the offer. Another year passed before she finally got the house, just a three-bedroomed council house, that she thought she and her family deserved. *We take care of what we value.* What bonds of care enabled this ordinary woman to value herself, her environment and her family so much that she went through three years of hell to get them a decent house? She would say that it was the memory of her mother, and what her mother had hoped for her that kept her going. Even if her society did not value her, her mother had, enough to give her the courage to care in a costly way.

Care is a somewhat loaded word at the moment. Link it with the word 'community' and you will evoke a wide range of responses, from outright hostility through deep cynicism to enthusiasm and concern. And yet it is an important word. It has two possible derivations, one from Old English meaning 'weighty' or 'grave', the other from the Latin *cara*, meaning 'dear' or 'precious', the same root from which we also derive charity, and that beautiful word found in the Scottish marriage service, cherish, to hold dear. Life comes through physical survival, but the good life comes from what we care about. Care is a state in which *something matters*. It is the opposite of apathy.

Care for other people is a state of recognition of another, a fellow-human being like oneself; of identification of one's self with the pain or joy of the other, of the awareness of a common humanity from which we all stem. That state we sometimes experience as a burden, sometimes as a delight. But *we take care of what we value.* We make an investment in it.

The urge to care

At the moment, a re-evaluation of the nature of care is taking place, both politically and culturally. Scotland is a small country, which still has quite a unitary sense. It is hard to go anywhere in Scotland without meeting someone who knows someone you know. And over the last couple of years, travelling the length and breadth of

Britain doing workshops on political and cultural identity with many different groups, it is my overwhelming experience that people care, and want to express their care. Or at least, they start off wanting to care. But the processes of care – the 'how' of care, is leaving too many people deeply frustrated in their attempts to care.

And here I find myself returning to Kenneth White's poem, quoted earlier in this book, where he talks of the question always being 'how'. And if meaning, belonging, identity, values are where we address 'how to select the features of real significance', then I think that care is where we begin to address 'how to order the signs and symbols so they will continue to form new patterns'. An ordering task is a political task, it is concerned with the body politic, with the ordering of civic society. You could say that the task of politics is our corporate care, how as a people we care for one another across a whole range of needs, from defence and relationships with other peoples to the health and education of the nation, to its support of those unable to support themselves. And the how of the political task is crucial. It is where the word becomes flesh, intentions become actions, theory becomes practice. *We take care of what we value.* But we need to know how best to do it.

Distorted processes ('hows') of care are both symptoms and causes of broken bonds of care, and of bonds being experienced not as links, connections and alliances, but as shackles. Frustrated carers, people become dis-abled, experience themselves as disem-powered and as valueless.

In recent years, the devaluing of local government by centralizing political tendencies has led to huge frustration among citizens and councillors alike. Add to this the fact that in many parts of the United Kingdom the dominance of one or another political party has led to carelessness towards constituents (if you know you are going to get elected anyway, it is very easy to take votes, and voters, for granted), and in some places to corruption and factional rivalry. This is a good recipe for widespread disillusionment and rejection of the whole process, as is seen in the low turnout polls for local government elections, in Glasgow, where I live, but in many other places too.

This is a disabling political process of care, breaking what was traditionally a strong bond in Scotland and elsewhere, the bond linking people into power through participation in political parties that represented their aspirations. But if political parties do not enable our care, why should we value them?

When people perceive themselves to be powerless to effect change, they respond in different ways. Sometimes they engage in struggling vertically against those in power. We know all about that in Scotland! In every election since 1979, Scots voted against Conservative government, and won the battle overwhelmingly – in Scotland. But the existing political processes continued to frustrate our care – and the bonds were further severed. The political differences that existed between Scotland and other parts of the UK were not sufficiently recognized. The 1997 General Election and subsequent referenda saw a massive shift in the political landscape, and constitutional change has been a vital part of that. With the election of a Scottish Parliament, the poss-ibility of new processes of care, of ordering the signs and symbols in ways that Scots feel are enabling rather than disabling has opened up. The task of revaluing local democracy also seems to be underway. It is to be fervently hoped that people can trust enough to make these steps work. We have already seen enough in Europe this century to last forever of the horrors of what can happen when people feel frustrated and disempowered in their political processes. If there is a political vacuum, a void of care, all too often 'identity' politics begins to re-emerge, with all its tribal baggage, to fill the vacuum. *If political systems do not enable our care, why should we value them?*

When the old bonds, the old loyalties, the old 'hows' fracture, new alliances are often formed. In politics, in campaigning activism, and of course in the church, this is always happening. But new bonds are fragile, sometimes too fragile. Tbe momentum slows, old dogmas reassert themselves, and, as often happens when people feel themselves frustrated vertically, they expressed their frustration horizontally. One can see this pattern in peace processes all over the world, not least in Northern Ireland. People who, in their values and concerns, have far more in common than what divides them, turn on each other in frustration, doing serious damage to tentative alliances in other areas. So they move from uniting where they can and dividing where they must (the ecumenical slogan) to dividing where they can and uniting hardly at all. This political collateral damage is not in essence any different from the man who degrades his family and environment because he can make no impact on the larger forces that disable his care. The same process is visible wherever we care to look, including in the church.

The horizontal aggression causes frustration all around. In politics, it strains the already strained relationship between party politics and campaigning or issue-based politics. In too many instances, campaigning politics are still seen as a secondary, even second-rate form of political engagement, and those who engage in them (very often the women, young people and marginalized groups missing from party politics) find themselves patronized or ignored by party politicians. Curiously enough, this pattern is also clearly evident in the church, where those on the margins of centralized authority, in house churches, issue groups and alternative communities (very often the women, young people and marginalized groups missing from official church bodies) find themselves patronized or ignored by church leaders.

The importance of a healthy and dynamic bond between the centre and the margins needs to be taken seriously. A healthy democracy, and a healthy church, recognize that people need to participate as well as be represented, especially given the increasing centralization of recent years. If prophetic action arises on the knife-edge of people's experience, the centre and the edge need to be connected by an artery that is pumping blood, not water. Because, *if political structures do not enable our alternative processes for care, why should we value them?*

In many parts of Britain, the severance of the bond between men and their communities is acute. It is the 'you'll be wanting the wife' syndrome familiar to community workers. There is given an impression of a weakening of the bonds of care that goes from the disabling of effective vertical action, through frustration expressed horizontally, to a place where care almost disappears. If you can't care, in the end you don't care. It is just too painful to have your efforts to care endlessly frustrated. Apathetic, you have no wishes, and without wish there is no will, political or personal.

The final severance of the bonds of care is when people not only stop caring for themselves, but inflict damage on themselves. I know a woman whose 22-year-old son, a gentle unemployed young man, had signed himself out of a drug release programme after two weeks. She met him, begging in the street. 'The children are killing themselves.'

One of the most agonized modern relationships in our culture seems to me to be that between distraught mothers and their self-damaging sons. I have met so many women who go through agonies of love, guilt, recrimination, impossibly painful 'how' choices of exclusion and support, and young men who are eaten up with shame and self-blame at what their mothers have suffered. Far from thinking that these young men do not care, I believe that they suffer at the acute end of care that has lost its traditional male means of expression – that of being wage-earners – and has found no other appropriate means of expression. Young women at least have an acceptable way of expressing care, however hard it is struggling to bring up children on income support. We take care of what we value.

For many women, living in an environment that not only is uncaring, that frustrates and fails to provide effective ways of allowing the expression of care, but is also often actively hostile, the alliances with other women are among the strongest and most effective. Here I am not just referring to explicitly feminist campaigning groups. I mean groups which arise where people are living on the knife-edge of experience: anti-poverty groups, housing groups, family support groups, groups for survivors of violence of one kind or another, drug release groups. On the margins of power these groups abound, where women can find a safe space to meet informally, mostly without much structure, where children are welcomed, where food can be bought cheaply, where stories can be told and heard without judgement. Women are highly active in co-operatives, in LETS (Local Exchange and Trading Schemes), in credit unions. In some ways, it almost resembles the nineteenth-century pattern of women, excluded from the formal political processes, organizing themselves in ways best suited to meeting their needs. Doing it for themselves!

Finding a voice

Activists and politicians and clergy sometimes bemoan the fact that in spite of all the efforts they make on people's behalf, they cannot get them out on the streets, they do not get the support their causes merit, they cannot get the people into the churches.

I do not think it is because people do not care. But if you have been devalued, ignored, talked for, talked about, talked at and talked down to for years, if your voice has been suppressed and you have been silenced, it takes a long time to find your voice again. I remember one man who had, somewhat reluctantly, come to spend a week in the MacLeod Centre on Iona, concerned with the future of Scotland. He came to every session of the week. He began on the outside of the circle, and gradually through the week drew his chair in closer. But for five days he said nothing, despite every encouragement. At 2 a.m. on the fifth day, he suddenly began to talk. He talked for three hours! He had had a difficult and disenfranchised life. But he certainly cared about Scotland.

New bonds of care are not forged overnight with good intentions and a politically correct agenda. They require weeks and months and years of attentiveness, of patience and respect and listening, and the willingness to open ourselves to being cared for. Most of our social and political processes simply do not or will not give that amount of time and of value to the forging of these bonds, this process that the Quakers call 'hearing people into speech'. Perhaps this is where women's alliances, which have been among the most enduring of new linkages, on a whole range of issues, political, social, spiritual, can teach us. Much of their strength comes from this willing embrace of the costs of relationality, and learning the 'how' of dialogue.

And we should be very clear in seeking new bonds about the extent to which people with some measure of empowerment (who may well include us) privilege their own agendas. I remember an environmental planning group which discontinued its local consultation process because it did not like what the people were saying! This is not dialogue. The church does not have a particularly good record in this respect, either in its relations with those outside the church, or, indeed, with its own marginalized members.

And we should be very cautious about taking on advocacy functions unless very specifically requested. Sometimes it is an unforgivable assumption. Sometimes speaking out for others is an attempt to assuage the discomfort of not being able or willing to speak out for ourselves! In any event, the most immediate thing is getting people together, creating a safe space. Mostly, given enough time, and a context where, temporarily at least, power imbalances are redressed, people can speak for themselves. But there are times when advocacy is necessary as a process of care, when for some reason or another people are prevented from expressing their own needs. I have found these guidelines to be helpful in advocacy:

- that there is a genuine mandate to do so directly from the people involved;

- that it is being undertaken because the people involved could not, despite all necessary efforts being made to support them in doing so;

- that it in no way reinforces the prevailing tendency to devalue the people's own contribution;

- that it is not a method of gaining personal status or recognition but is designed to elicit some concrete change in the situation.

Dialogue, advocacy, building new alliances, creating new bonds of care: all of these things require great sensitivity and finessing. It is fatally easy for care to be seen as control, as patronage, as manipulation, as many things it is not intended to be. Therefore it matters how we give care – and also how we receive it. There is an art of giving and receiving to learn.

I heard a rather sad story recently about the giving of a gift which had gone terribly wrong. An elderly couple had received a visit from the minister of the church they were members of. Among their possessions they had an embroidered tapestry of the Last Supper, which had been sewn by a relative of theirs, long since dead. They had decided they would like to make a gift of this tapestry to their church, and had even picked out the spot in the church where they felt it should hang.

However, the minister, though thanking them for the thought, refused to accept the offer. He explained his reasons – the tapestry was not in keeping with the style of the building, and would not fit in with the other art in the church. Furthermore if he accepted this gift, then many other people might also want to give gifts of art which might be inappropriate, and he did not wish to set a precedent. He declined the gift with thanks.

The elderly couple were hurt and offended by this refusal – so deeply offended, in fact, that from that time, about a dozen years ago, to this, they had refused to set foot in the church again. They simply stopped going, though they had not joined any other church. Now the wife was seriously ill, and longing to receive home communion. But they were not prepared to ask the minister into their home. And though the minister had made many efforts to heal the rift, they had all been unsuccessful.

In this sad little story, it is easy to feel sympathetic to all parties – the elderly couple wishing to give something cherished to their church, and feeling, when their gift was rejected, that somehow they had also been rejected. When we give a gift, we give a little of ourselves. But one can also feel sympathy with the minister. I do not suppose there are many of us who have not received a gift from a well-meaning relative which has made us groan inwardly and frantically think where we can put it where it will be most out of sight. And for the minister, the stakes were much higher.

And what the story does remind us of is the fact that the whole business of giving and receiving is really quite a delicate one, in which we must tread softly. There seems to be an art in giving and receiving.

We know the appropriate and welcome gift from our own experience; we try to follow the same principles in our own giving. We value:

- something given where the giver has consulted us about what we would really like;
- or, unable to do that directly, has sought to discover from those close to us what would be useful, delightful, helpful to us;
- something given with sensitivity, where the gift is not so extravagant, either materially or emotionally, that its cost would embarrass us because we could never give a similar gift in return; but not something so cheap that we feel insulted along with the gift. And not something that we sense is given along with a clear message of patronage and the expectation of moral pay-off. There is a kind of unspoken law of equivalence, of reciprocity, at work here.

Such gifts we welcome, and have little difficulty receiving. How interesting to discover, then, that so much of the giving and receiving in the Gospels seems to break all the codes of good practice. We find Jesus being the recipient of extravagant, hugely costly, and to all intents and purposes quite inappropriate gifts:

- a collection of strange and rather unsuitable gifts for a baby;
- an extravagant and quite disproportionate personal gesture from a woman who anointed him, a gesture obviously highly embarrassing to everyone else;
- hospitality very possibly purchased with ill-gotten gains, the proceeds of corruption and extortion, given by criminals and social outcasts.

What are we to make of these gifts, who might well have sympathy with Judas' question – 'Why wasn't this money used for the poor?' (John 12.4–5) – if not with his motivation?

Jesus gave gifts too, as well as receiving them. There are quite a few stories about widows in the Gospels. The one, for instance, of a poor widow in a place called Nain, grieving the loss of her only son, her sole support. For a widowed woman in a society without social security and widows' pensions, the other male members of the family were her first recourse – brothers, nephews, but above all, sons. Without these, she would have no way of keeping herself. In both her personal and her political economy, the widow of Nain had lost that which was of great value. In the story, Jesus raises her son from the dead, and gives him back to his mother. Again in the pursuit of good practice, one might question this giving. Had Jesus given to one person in the community something that might lead to envy and division, something that others might want? Were there, perhaps, other widows in Nain?

And another widow, Mary, stands beside the cross, watching her son die. There is an irony here – this is one mother whose son Jesus could not save. John, the disciple whom Jesus loved, was standing with her – and Jesus, on the cross, gave them to each other. Was this the gift they wanted? I cannot imagine that it was – each of them wanted him. Did he ask them what they wanted? He simply gave.

Realistically, our experience of giving and receiving is much more of having to engage with the givenness of something rather than of receiving a welcome gift; and the givenness is often not one we welcome. We confront the givenness of mortality, of injustice, of seemingly intractable circumstances. We experience the givenness of pain. Where is the art in receiving these? Where is the art in giving them, which we also have complicity in?

In giving and receiving we are participating in a transaction, an exchange. Perhaps the art lies not so much in the giving or receiving as in the capacity to transform the exchange, to bring out of the transaction something new, something unexpected, something previously hidden. I see Jesus effecting this transformation in these exchanges with widows, as in so many.

'Jesus gave him back to his mother' (Luke 7.15). This is for me one of the most beautiful sentences in the Bible. Essentially, this transaction is a restoration. To the widow of Nain, Jesus restores:

• her personal economy, this beloved person of absolute worth;

- the political economy in which she dwelt, her means of material support (Jesus never separates the personal and the political);
- her relationship, her human community;
- her love, and hence her hope.

To restore a person's child – what greater gift can there be? And for Mary and John also, a transformation:

- the restoration, the redirection of the capacity to love, the transformation of the personal;
- the restoration of the necessary material provision, the transformation of the political;
- the restoration into relationship in the human community, in a new form of kinship.

Again and again we see it, this transformation of the transaction, and always at the heart of it the restoration of community, the new relationship, the new covenant:

- a new relationship for the men who brought gifts for a king and found a child born outside the palace;
- a new relationship for criminals and outcasts;
- a new relationship for the women who financed Jesus;
- a new relationship for the woman who anointed Jesus, who, her gift received with grace, henceforth will be known not for the greatness of her sins but for the greatness of her love.

Always a new relationship of restoration into the human community being created in the transformation of the exchange. And conversely, we see also the refusal of transformation, of Jesus' offered gift of restoration in an inclusive human community – 'Thank God I am not like these others', said the Pharisee in the temple (see Luke 18.11). But this is both given and gift – 'by the grace of God, I am part of these others'.

I find myself so often unable to control the nature of the exchanges I participate in – they are given transactions – that all I can do is seek ways for their transformation, for restoration into relationship. The text in Luke speaks of Jesus' heart being filled with compassion for the widow. In the midst of a large crowd, he saw the person. There is a word, 'enthusiasm', which comes from the Greek, and it means to be possessed or inspired by the god – whether of love or anger, of compassion or courage. Jesus was an enthusiast. I think that perhaps part of what it means to be an artist of giving and receiving is to be open to this inspiration. In our different ways, as followers of Jesus, we are enthusiasts, we have been possessed by God, filled with care. This gift of enthusiasm, the sense that this, what we do as the church, in bearing witness and in care, in some way matters, however inadequately we may feel we do it; it is reciprocal, it is an exchange one to another.

> From you I receive, to you I give;
> together we learn, and so we live.

The disciples of Jesus, struggling with new concepts of care, of a new, inclusive community, were full of questions; and 'how' was the most urgent of them. The major part of the existence and experience of any community, including the resurrection community that is called the church, is taken up with the question 'how'. How shall we organize, how shall we proceed, how shall we decide? When we hear people asking themselves many of the questions that we have asked, there is always a temptation to want to say, 'You want to know how! I'll tell you!' And of course, it would be the wrong answer, because the 'how' is always responsive to context, to a particular task, place and situation. The questions may be the same, but the answers are always nuanced.

Invited to list what, for them, were the main characteristics in caring, one group came up with these suggestions:

- group unity
- shared responsiveness
- preserving the challenge
- shutting up and listening
- lateral thinking
- different ways of approach
- allowing leadership
- shifting leadership
- recognizing varying skills and abilities
- recognizing limitations
- humour
- preserving dignity
- simplifying obstacles
- collective action

- looking at options
- allowing personal choice
- mutual trust
- non-abusive power
- non-exclusive recognition of difficulty
- questioning validity of course
- individual responsibility in expressing need clearly
- action rather than theory
- one obstacle at a time
- taking care of yourself in order to be able to take care of others

Of course, on one level, these considerations are diverse, not necessarily coherent, not even always consistent with one another. But more profoundly, they are a way of saying that in caring 'we need to have processes, and not just goals, which we can trust'. 'How' is a process question, 'how' is a journey.

We cannot write other people's answers for them. But we can recognize hints, pointers, signposts on the journey. Not long ago I was travelling by train, and the train got stuck just south of Wigan for the best part of two hours. Having read my own newspaper from cover to cover, and even attempted the crossword, in desperation I picked up a *Daily Telegraph* (not a paper I often read) which someone had left lying about. And in it, I read a story which made a deep impression on me.

> In Cambodia
> women pick their way through minefields.
> They have been trained by aid workers
> in the useful domestic skill
> of defusing landmines.
>
> Working in teams of twenty,
> they can clear an acre
> in two months.
> Inch
> by
> inch.
>
> Naturally, there are accidents.
> A foot here,
> a hand there,
> or a life.

But they don't have any choice.
They need the land
to feed their children.

(KG, 'de-contamination', 1997)

I find in this story some pointers to the gospel 'how', the 'how' for communities of hope.

I see people engaging with reality, with the situation as it really is, in all its flaws and all its dangers and all its injustices, rather than operating out of some illusory picture of the way they think it should be.

I see people working as a team, co-operating, depending on one another. No troubleshooters here, no individual heroes dropping out of the sky by parachute to save the rest.

I see people working to bring life out of death, not with violence, but with the peacemakers' commitment to non-violence.

I see people proceeding with infinite patience, slowly, inch by inch, resisting the temptation to take anything for granted, not moving until they are sure that the ground has cleared, with great attention to detail.

I see people acting with sensitivity, using their senses and intuition, listening to the ground, observing closely the slightest movement or irregularity in the earth; and gently, delicately, not poking and prodding with a big stick which might detonate an explosion.

I see people being ready to learn, to be trained, and to use the right tools for the job.

I see people prepared to work where they can best be used – as toolmakers, suppliers, trainers or sweepers.

I see people who are prepared to take the risks, who know that there is danger involved, and that there will be a cost.

I see people who, while concentrating on the mines, also have a vision of the field as it might be – beautiful and fruitful.

I see people for whom feeding their children, working for the future, is not just a choice but a necessity. People who care.

In the 'how' of this fearful task, these women are bearing witness to the victory of life over death. They are a community of the resurrection.

'How to order the signs and the symbols'. It is in this ordering task that we most act as people made in the image of God, that we take upon ourselves participation in the divine ordering that is part of what it is to be human. But because we are not God, it is where we need most humility, most capacity for self-awareness and critique, and most capacity to seek forgiveness and be open to change. Only a very thin line divides ordering from controlling. In this, I find it helpful to keep going back to look at the nature of God's ordering.

I am someone who by temperament is somewhat resistant to control, and it is easy for me to think of order in less than enthusiastic terms, to see it as what is tame, dull, predictable, unadventurous. So it is good for me to stand on a cliff on the west coast of Scotland looking out at the Atlantic Ocean and see the wildness of the waters, the surging power of the waves, to feel the wind and to delight in the vivid colours, and know that this is also part of God's ordering. And to remember that God's ordering is many things:

- it is diverse: from the placid, gentle and fruitful to the wild and adventurous, to the barren and seemingly unyielding rock;
- it is dynamic: a continual exchange, a dialectic of creative energy, responsive and interconnected;
- it always goes beyond our blueprint: it includes what is odd, humorous, apparently flawed or imperfect;
- it involves pain and a continuous process of dying to ourselves and being born again into a larger whole;
- it has a certain ruthlessness, requiring us to be channels of its birth, regardless of our bruised or complaining egos;
- it holds the capacity for surprise: we never know everything, and we do not order alone, but with others, who bring their insights and perceptions to enlarge and surprise us.

'How' invites us into a different way of seeing. In spite of everything, care persists. The urge and desire to care are still enormously strong. There are many thousands of caring groups in Britain, of people who care about their neighbourhoods, about housing, about health and physical and mental well-being, about the environment, about the arts – the list is long. Many of the old bonds of care are still powerful, many new bonds have been created. But they do not yet constitute a strategy for justice. Severance and separation are acute. Some important bonds still need to be forged. I believe that the most important alliances to be made are between those groups, organizations and persons who affirm the intrinsic worth of all, and consequent value for all. In a free market economy and its underlying spirituality, where value is added extrinsically, from outside market forces, resistance to a politics driven by economics cannot come from the economic, it can only come from the cultural and the spiritual. Only the cultural and spiritual can empower the struggle to live as subject, because in the economic, we are all object.

This means that we have to enter into alliances that cut across old allegiances, and be very open about it. Values show up in what people do, not what they say. In making new alliances, perhaps the criterion 'by their fruits ye shall know them' (Matthew 7.20, AV) needs to be rigorously applied. It is the one applied by those whose care is at present frustrated, distorted and deadened by our present processes. And we are all losers in that.

7

One – But Which One?
A Question of Difference

A few years ago, I was watching a late-night television news programme. It was an interview with the eminent Canadian economist, J. K. Galbraith, and as he outlined his theory of the culture of contentment, much of which I was in agreement with, I became aware of another thought breaking the surface of my consciousness as I gazed in admiration at this distinguished and immaculately turned-out giant of twentieth-century ideas. 'I wonder whether he irons his own shirts.'

Now I should make it clear immediately that this was not some feminist moan. It was a genuinely curious speculation, an indicator of a basically trivial and unserious mind, some might say, but certainly evidence of one of the many strands of preoccupation of my existence. Laundry has occupied a considerable part of my time since I became an adult – collecting it, sorting it, washing it, drying it, folding it, and even ironing it in the days before I abandoned ironing to those for whom it was a priority! A spell living on the Indian Ocean island of Mauritius, bereft of washing-machine and laundrette, simply made me more aware of the fact that in the scale of women washing worldwide, I had it easy. Although, in common with the vast majority of the population, I have never been able to afford to pay someone else to do my washing, at least I do not have to do it in the river. As I watched these women gather by the river with their huge bundles (and it was all women) I had an acute realization of the sheer amount of time involved in the children emerging from township shacks, overcrowded tenements and pavement benders in their spotless white socks or saris.

So laundry has gradually become for me not just a given of my life, but the symbol of a larger given. It is a symbol that stands for shopping and cooking and cleaning, for doctor's appointments and trips to the seaside, for visits to relatives and letters to friends. It stands for the anguished late-night phone conversations about relationships in crisis and for the early-morning distress call of a neighbour having a nervous breakdown. It stands for the local campaign to get the drug dealers off the streets or the dangerous part of the river fenced in. It is the PTA and the church council, it is the increasingly fragile and confused elderly relative, it is birthdays and anniversaries and holidays and that thing that incorporates so many of these others, the ever-expanding marketing opportunity known as Christmas, now generally regarded much as one might a military campaign.

Laundry has become for me a symbol of what are, quite literally, my *pre-occupations*, those things which I do before and alongside and beyond what might legitimately be termed my occupation, my work, that which I am paid for, or which resources and furthers the work I am paid for.

But most of all, it is a symbol of the fact that the context of my life and my work is one of community. I begin everything in relationship. It is the underlying fact of my existence. In the midst of relationship to family, friends, neighbours, neighbourhood, church and beyond, I attempt to carve out some degree of autonomy. I try to find 'a room of my own'. I endeavour to be single-minded, to hush the babble of voices chattering on about laundry and running out of toilet paper and making a cake for my sister's birthday, and largely it works. Well, at least, what is as likely to happen now is that I check out someone else's shopping in the supermarket queue because I am engrossed in a conversation in my head about tomorrow's work meeting, as happened to me recently. At least, now, all my voices are in dialogue. The laundry is the raw material of theological reflection. I make a virtue out of necessity.

This peculiar state of mind which our information technology society has helpfully labelled multi-tasking is, of course, not peculiar to me alone. It is the experience of most women, and a smaller number of men. Historically, it has always been the experience of women to be the primary carer: of children, of the elderly, of the most vulnerable in society; to be the connectors, the go-betweens, the glue that joins human beings together in community. But this century has seen the project of 'a room of one's own' become that not just of small numbers of women, but of millions. Of course, carving out that autonomous space was far from unknown in past centuries. I think of Jane Austen, writing her notebooks in secret in the midst of family life; of the Brontes, George Eliot and the others for whom a male pseudonym became the autonomous space; of the women further back in the Middle Ages, who found it in enclosure in a convent or cell: Julian of Norwich, Hildegarde of Bingen, Teresa of Avila and many less well known. Today, in parts of the world, though not only the Christian world, women find their own room within the veil. Others, like the Welsh farmer's wife Ann Griffiths, found it in mysticism. For many women it was a dangerous and dark struggle. For some, the struggle led to accusations of madness, for too many of them a room of one's own ended up being bedlam, the asylum. For a million women in Europe it led to witchcraft trials, torture and death.

Still, however creative or costly their struggles, these were the exception rather than the rule. For most women, the reality of being the makers and repairers of community was all that there was; the voices of children, relatives, neighbours and the men who had to be looked after and heeded left little or no space to find one's own voice. Only in prayer or dreaming or imagination was it really safe to draw the lines that say: 'So far, and no farther. Beyond here is private, inviolate, virgin territory.' Other than that, it was woman's duty, and supposed to be her delight, to merge, to blend in, to allow, to suffer, to have the lines drawn for her and, when necessary, to permit the lines to be blurred, or even obliterated. If one wants to look to the Bible for evidence, what better example than that of Mary the mother of Jesus. It is announced to her what will happen in the most profoundly personal space a woman has, which is not just her womb but her understanding of its meaning, her own room. Like so many women before and since, her best choice is to embrace that willingly. It is the only exercise of her personhood she has left, this voluntary self-surrender.

That it is in so many circumstances a delight should not be overlooked or denied. That our contribution to, and part in the well-being of others offers considerable satisfaction, feelings of value, identity, belonging, continuity and just a lot of pure pleasure is not said as much as it perhaps should be. It is the other side of the demand, the anxiety, the frustration and the sheer exhaustion. Its absence is sorely felt. Returning briefly to laundry, I remember years ago, in the early days of my marriage (when I still ironed, when I was still married), standing in the kitchen ironing my husband's shirts. A friend who was visiting, a woman in her thirties, unmarried and living alone, rather wistfully expressed her envy of my domestic task. Slightly incredulous, I immediately offered her the iron, and as she pressed and folded perfectly, she said, 'At least somebody needs you.' What for me at that time was perceived as a duty, in her eyes seemed a delight. Such yearning is never deserving of scorn. It is never really a yearning to iron.

It is part of being human to desire to merge, to drop our boundaries, to come together in unity, to be as one. But in the twentieth century, 'which one?' has become an important question. For a long time the dominant map, the prevailing world-view, has been that of those who shared the dominant identity. Those who drew the maps of what it meant to be sucessfully and fully human were mostly male, white, European (particularly Anglo-Saxon), Christian, powerful (by means of their wealth, their class, their education, their military capacity) and heterosexual. In the church, those who drew the maps were also clerical. They were the ones who selected the features of real significance for the others. Projected from where they were, it is hardly surprising that the blueprint for the human being looked remarkably similar. It was after all, made in their image. Even information that contradicted that image could be reshaped. Jesus of Nazareth was a Middle-Eastern Jewish Semite. The likelihood of him having had blond hair and blue eyes was fairly remote. But there are still adults in this generation who remember the pictures of the fair, white Jesus of their Sunday School childhoods, fully dressed, with little naked black babies tumbling around his knee appealing for British pennies to help them. The subliminal message is unmistakable to us now.

For centuries, when people have merged their boundaries to become one, there was no real question about 'which one'. For women, it was the man. For non-whites, non-Europeans, non-Christians, for those without power or status, for the homosexual, the model of what they should aspire to was equally clear. And if it was not possible to become that, then they should serve it, as the superior model. The interests of the woman would be subordinated to those of the man, of the black man to the white, of the poor to the rich, and so on. Though self-interest, aggrandizement and the lust for wealth and power have driven the colonization and imperialism of Europe since the Middle Ages, the effortless assumption of superiority was an adequate justification for invasion, land appropriation and dispossession, plunder and slavery.

The fact that there have always been exceptions to the rule of 'which one' – the egalitarian communities like the Society of Friends, the missionaries who saw the people to whom they had been 'sent' as equals and not inferiors, the individuals who overcame their inferior status to rise to power – is no great comfort. Many of them met the same fate as those with whom they had identified: insecurity, persecution, powerlessness and death when they threatened the interests of the dominant power. For millions, 'a room of one's own', the right to have inviolable self-determined space, *the right to be different* without being oppressed for one's difference, remained a distant dream.

But we are women and men of our time, and our time, on the threshold of a new millennium, is democratic. We live in a country, and in an era, where democracy is the prevailing political idea, and for this I am profoundly grateful. It has been important beyond compare for me as a woman, and for millions, both women and men, across the globe. Though it is an idea which is often found wanting in practice, and though it is not the experience of many parts of the world, it is one which, thousands of years after its birth, has worked its way into human consciousness enough to become both an aspiration and an ideal for much of humanity. It is enshrined in legislation, in UN charters and in human rights declarations at every level.

So even where it is absent in practice, and even where it is opposed outright, the notion of human rights, of the equality of all persons of every gender, race, class and status, of their dignity and personhood, is shaping both our individual consciousness and our world-view. One of the fundamental consequences of democracy is that it gives to every person the right to be the subject of their own lives – to own their lives, if you like. And the corollary of that right of the individual is that it be the same for every other individual. We have the right to be subject up to and until it interferes with that right for others. Our responsibility in a democracy is to safeguard that right as much for others as we do for ourselves. The two are one and the same. The one is the guarantor of the other.

We go
as far as we are able,
or, as far as we are allowed,

whichever is further.
Then we push a little
(just testing!).
When we meet resistance,
real resistance
(not the playful kind that says,
'go on, I really want you
to push a little harder'),
then we stop.
We understand,
so far,
but no further.
And there,
we draw the lines,
boundaries,
borders.
To cross would be
encroachment,
stepping out of line.
This is the land we must live in.

(KG, 'drawing the lines of engagement', 1997)

This century has seen a great redrawing of the lines, a claiming or reclaiming of territory, of the right to be different. My reflections on occupation and pre-occupation are a part of my own engagement in redrawing lines concerning the role and status of women. This is a worldwide engagement, though it operates in different contexts and with different goals in various parts of the world. Commentators who see it as essentially a Western notion, concerned with such trivial concerns as the desegregation of the MCC and the shattering of the 'glass ceiling' preventing more women from becoming economic high-fliers, are simply ignorant of the extent to which economic injustice, participation in decision-making, violence against women, access to education and health and a whole range of other issues are high on the agenda of women in practically every country in the world. Many of these are not the liberal democracies of the West, and the lines may not be being redrawn in the same way as they have been here; but being redrawn they certainly are, and will continue to be so.

This is, I think, an irreversible movement. It affects things as basic as the ability of women whose men have been killed in war to support their dependants. In a country like Afghanistan, where basic freedoms for women such as the freedom to receive health care have been brutally removed, the scale of repression of women is on a par with slavery. Though it is hard to imagine that quite so much complicity with this repression would have happened if it had been directed at men, nevertheless there is widespread international revulsion at it. The lines have been redrawn about what is acceptable treatment of women, and the forcible attempt by the Taliban to push women back into the old lines by force and coercion points up acutely how much they have changed.

But of course it is not only women who have been redrawing the lines. One of the most visible demonstrations of this has been in the decolonization of countries formerly part of European empires. The last fifty years have seen the reclaiming of well over half the world, from India, the 'jewel in the crown' of the British Empire, to the break-up of the Russian-dominated Soviet Union.

Some of that reclamation has been peaceful, some has been only at the cost of bloody wars of independence. And yet, so much has consciousness shifted that in countries which only one generation ago were lamenting the loss of their empires, it now seems incredible and embarrassing that we should have so presumed. Many of these now independent countries are still disentangling the knots caused by European line-drawing which overrode ancient tribal identities and shunted whole peoples around continents like pieces on a chessboard.

Racism too has increasingly become a point of awareness of changing lines. Not that it does not still exist, hugely, sometimes consciously, sometimes quite unconsciously the attitudes of the old maps still persisting. But its enshrinement in oppressive laws is more and more being challenged and overturned, and the law is more and more called upon to deliver justice.

'Removing all traces of racism from our relationships means affirming that we are different and that we shall remain different' (Edgar Pisani). I think this is true not only of racism, but of any context in which oppressive or coercive behaviour is based on the assumption that others should think like us, act like us, do what we wish, for therein lies their salvation. It may be nearer to the truth that actually we want people to agree with us because therein lies *our* salvation. If they accept our view of things, if they become part of us, then they will accept our economic agenda, our political agenda, our language, our culture, they will support the right cricket team, eat the right food, adopt our customs. They will reinforce our religious beliefs by making them theirs.

But in the century of democracy, we cannot any longer impose conformity by the use of coercive or oppressive behaviour. It is true that international opinion and practice is still grossly inconsistent about this: for every action against a Saddam Hussein rolling over the lines of Kuwait, there is an inaction against equally culpable invasion and violation of territorial integrity. Self- and national interest is still a determining factor, though now its terms of reference are economic rather than political. But whether the boundary dispute is between countries or between neighbours at odds with one another over the garden fence, the issue is similar. It is about the right to be different, up to the point where that interferes with the right of another to be different, and about where that point comes.

It is a difficult thing to allow others the right to be different. It can make us feel uncomfortable, even threatened. It upsets our preconceived notions about the way things are, offers us new information that we are not sure we want to take in. Often the perceived sense of threat we feel is out of all proportion to its actual extent. The threat people often feel when confronted by beggars or homeless people is not logical, on one level. These are mostly people with nothing, no status, no influence, above all, no power. Yet they are routinely vilified and often beaten up, just for existing. Why should we feel such a sense of threat from them? But on another level they confront us with things we would rather not think about: our embarrassment at their homelessness, our deepest fears of failure, our own better-disguised chaos. Rather than admit these things as part of us, it is easier, less uncomfortable, to project them on to the one who has awakened them in us, who has disturbed our sleeping demons. Better to see these people as demons, rather than as persons.

Sometimes the perceived threat is the result of sheer ignorance. We are so attached to what we know, so keen to project that on to the world around us, that we are often blind to the huge extent of what we do not know.

The map of the new country
If we are going to a new country, to work, say, or as a volunteer, or

simply as a visitor, it is a useful exercise to put up a map of the place, then to make a list of all the things we know about it – for example its climate, language, religion, economy, political and cultural institutions, customs and so on. We may know quite a lot, especially if we have been reading up on it, or if we have actually visited it already, or know people who live there.

Then we might make another list, this time of all the things we do not know about the country. Even if we have a lot of factual information, there will be a great deal we are ignorant of; it may well be in the area of customs, values, relationships, expectations, all the intangible and often invisible factors that nevertheless are crucial to the social fabric of any country.

What we know about the place we are going to will always be less than what we do not know. If we do not speak the language, this will be an additional barrier which must be crossed in some way – even if we have the blithe native English-speaker's assumption that the rest of the world will negotiate that barrier on our behalf by speaking our language. In any case, we will have to rely very much on our hosts in the project, whether they be employers, colleagues, tour guides or friends. We will have some significant areas of dependency, and will need interpreters, not just of language but of the culture and country in general. Therefore, we cannot go in the style of those conveying favours.

One of the features which characterize maps is that they mark out the boundaries which separate one country, territory, region, geographical zone from another. These boundaries may be physical: mountain ranges, rivers, seas, deserts, plains. They may be political: the borders and buffer zones which define one country as being not another country. They say to us, here and no further is where this country, terrain or territory runs to.

Such boundaries are relatively clear to find and see (though visitors in foreign lands sometimes unwittingly cross borders and find themselves in physical or political difficulty). But countries also have invisible boundaries, of culture, custom, religion and expectation. These too say, here and no further is where you may go. It is far easier, albeit unwittingly, to transgress these boundaries.

Westerners are used to a great deal of freedom with regard to boundaries. From childhood through adolescence to adulthood we have increasing freedom to travel, to be mobile socially and geographically, to cross many boundaries, to push or test the limits of these. Only poor people in our country do not have these freedoms – though, ironically, it is also increasingly the case that the freedom of children to play, to move about within the environs of their own homes, is being threatened by the adult freedom to travel, as road traffic reaches the proportions where it is not safe to let children out to play.

Other countries and cultures may have very different boundaries. Mobility may be much more restricted. Family relationships and roles may be much more defined (the adolescent rebellion is by no means a worldwide phenomenon). Social and political freedoms may be more curtailed. Attitudes to privacy and personal space may be very varied. Some cultures will find it hard to believe that anyone enjoys solitude, because they are intensely communitarian, and out of the very best of motives will not let you be alone. There will be differences of working practices, of attitudes to authority and older people, to personal behaviour and gender attitudes.

On the other hand, there may be areas of life in which we have explored much less, and are less free, than in the host country. These might include things like community, spirituality, relationship with the environment, creativity and survival skills. We may find that our experience has been both freer and more restricted.

Such differences in boundaries are not necessarily right or wrong. They are simply different. While visiting another country, we can recognize the necessity of respecting these differences, as the ways of a house in which we are guests in our own country are respected. Judgements, if they must be made (and judgements are not the same as preferences), need to be reserved for a later time, when we have had the opportunity to observe, to listen, to learn and to reflect, and when we are back in our own place.

Visiting a foreign country is an experience which inevitably brings what is new, different and strange with it. No amount of preparation can really tell us what it will be like, how it will make us feel. And when travelling, there is no substitute for an open mind. However many maps we have, and however much we have studied them, in the end we find ourselves exploring what is for us uncharted land, the land of our own new experience. But maps are not territory, only what we know so far. So we go prepared to revise our maps, and to suspend our biases and prejudices. Rather than becoming angry or frustrated by what we cannot do, we explore what it is like to live within other boundaries, and encounter a wealth of new experience. When we travel in a new country, we expect it to be different, and we are happy that it is so; indeed, that is a primary purpose in visiting it (unless we are among those who really only want an exact replica of life at home, except with better weather). Indeed, we may regret these things that seem to us too familiar, too like the things we find at home. We affirm that we are different, and that we shall remain different.

So why should we not have the same expectations, the same openness, when we are encountering the new country that is a different gender, a different race, a different religion, a different culture or way of being, a different tribal identity. All of these inhabit a particular inner geography, with their own distinctive features, landmarks, signposts. All of them have their own borders. All of them require interpretation to the outsider. Their language may require translation. These geographies of the spirit may in many respects look similar, even identical to ours – but they may be understood very differently. We cannot assume we understand the meaning of something just because it looks familiar. We have to ask questions, listen, observe. We cannot draw conclusions based on our own experience about the experience of others. We cannot conclude, for example, that just because we have never had a bad experience with the police, anyone who says they have is automatically a troublemaker, to be mistrusted. Years of living in an inner-city housing estate have taught me that the hard way. Sometimes just being poor is enough to make you a target. But nor will I assume that the police are automatically to be mistrusted. The same years taught me that too.

When we encounter people who are different, we can do so aggressively, armed with all our prejudices, assumptions and biases. Or we can assume a posture of guarded neutrality. Or we can see it as an opportunity for dialogue and exchange. There is a sense in which every meeting between two people is a dialogue of civilizations. We bring whole worlds with us, each one our history, geography, identity, values, our own experience and memory. True dialogue is not possible where we simply want to talk without listening, to give answers without asking questions. Our identity, including our Christian identity, is surely not very securely rooted and grounded if it cannot stand exposure to questioning, to other ideas, experiences, ways of being.

There is a member of the Iona Community, a practising Christian called Stanley Hope. He lives in Rochdale, where for many years he was the Community Relations Officer. His life is dedicated to dialogue with Muslims. He has learned Urdu, the mother tongue of many of them, has shared hospitality and food in their homes and his, has identified with their struggles, has campaigned against unjust and discriminatory immigration laws. Recently, he wrote in *Coracle*, the magazine of the Iona Community:

> Ramadhan is here once again, and another year has flown. Dialogue, I have learned, is much more than the dead end where the concentration on theology often leads. It brings friendship, which in turn leads to understanding and trust. It is a permanent state, in which imagination, trust and courage can grow and which makes action on social justice possible. When we know and trust each other I have often been surprised at what becomes possible to discuss and do together. Srangely enough, in many of our meetings and conversations the teaching of Jesus has come alive.
>
> In the Muslim people I have found friendship, kindness, hospitality, generosity, respect for others, a deep sense of humanity and compassion and a concern for justice.
>
> I remain grateful that my life has been enriched beyond measure. It has been a journey that I would not have missed for anything.

The church has not got a very good record on dialogue. It is often not comfortable letting people be different. In the past, it has killed people rather than let them be different. We can sometimes barely be in dialogue with our fellow Christians. There are many within the number of those who claim Christian identity who only recognize as Christians at all those who think like them, practise like them and, often, look like them. We are still remarkably wedded to the notion that being a Christian is a matter of assent to a set of propositions, the ability to give the correct formula, the right answers to a series of definitive questions, and to do all that in a particular language or code, and not a relationship with and to Jesus Christ. We would never expect or imagine that all our relationships would follow a particular blueprint – indeed, their diversity is part of their attraction. So why should we expect it of this relationship?

Not long ago, I was invited to speak to a group of students training for ordination in a Scottish theological college. Given the freedom to choose what I would talk about, I elected to do so on ecumenism, a subject on which I have some enthusiasm and a lot of experience. Having heard me out politely, they then began to quiz me on the doctrinal purity of my views. Surely there were parts of the dogma and practice of other denominations that I found in error, even possibly dangerous or heretical? I forebore to reply that I found that to be true of all denominations, including theirs and my own. Surely there had to be an irreducible core of beliefs, that you could draw a line around, so that you could be sure who was in and who was out? Without questioning their eager assumption that theirs was the line that was in the right place, I attempted to say that for me ecumenism, indeed, Christian faith itself, was not a question of uniformity of belief. In fact, I *assume* difference, it is my starting point. I have never met two Christians who agree on every single doctrinal point – even if their propositions are the same, their understanding of these, and the meanings they hold, may be significantly different. Assuming difference, for me what matters is that we still love each other, respect each other, listen to each other, remain in dialogue. We are, after all, at the very least, neighbours. I am not sure whether they heard me.

Richard Holloway, describing the difference between a sect and a church, says that a sect breaks away, it *dis-sects* itself to maintain its doctrinal purity, its uniformity. Having done so once, it is then faced with the temptation (when difference arises, as it invariably will) to go on dividing into smaller and smaller sects in order to maintain that purity. A glance at Scottish church history demonstrates that very clearly. But the church is *a community of conflict*. It affirms that we are different, and that we will remain different, but we will still be in community, we will still love each other. Unity is not the same as uniformity. It is something much more demanding, but also much more rewarding than that. It is the embracing of difference in a unity that depends on inclusion and not exclusion. The image of the Trinity, the three-in-one, the community of God, is for me the pattern of our unity. We are many, we are one.

The church, fragmented and excluding, can go in two directions. It can further exclude, draw the lines more narrowly and firmly, be sectarian. It can be, literally, dia-bolic, that which severs, separates, hurls apart. Or it can be inclusive, draw its lines more broadly and softly, be communitarian. It can be sym-bolic, that which heals, unites, draws together. That is why, for me, 'which one?' is the *ecumenical* one, the one that is also the many. The Celtic symbol for the Trinity is a three-leafed shape, each leaf quite distinct, but drawn with one unbroken line which flows through each, intersecting so that it forms an unending unity.

What I observe about Jesus is that his exchanges with the people he met were all about including those who were excluded. He met them as persons, and the transaction drew them into community. He met a lot of people who were considered quite unacceptable in the religious and cultural orthodoxy – because they were foreigners, criminals, cheats, prostitutes, because they were deranged or poor or wounded or suffering from disability or disease. To meet them, he willingly crossed the boundaries of what was familiar and respectable and safe. He asked questions a lot. He asked people what they wanted him to do for them, rather than telling them. He recognized the need that people had for a room of their own: a space for Mary to learn, a space for the man possessed to be safe, a space for the Samaritan woman to express her thoughts, a space for people to make mistakes and fail. He asked things of them too: a drink of water from a well, hospitality in the house of one shunned for his fraudulent practices; and accepted the gifts people gave him.

One of my favourite stories is the one about the Syrophoenician woman (Matthew 15.21–8; Mark 7.24–30), a foreigner, who came to ask Jesus to heal her sick daughter when he was visiting her territory to get away for a little from the danger that was now pursuing him and, presumably, to get a little peace and quiet. Some Christians go into paroxysms of re-interpretation and pietizing in order to avoid the unavoidable fact that in this story, Jesus does not show up in a good light. A visitor in her country, he is insulting to her people in a way that nowadays would be deemed quite explicitly racist. But I like the story precisely because in it, he acts like a man of his time and place, with the cultural baggage of any human being. When the woman challenges him, he has the openness to look at his behaviour, to see the assumptions in it, and to go beyond it. He recognizes the necessity to venture beyond the lines. He has the courage and humility to learn and to change. I do not find much hope for change or salvation in impossibly inhuman perfection. But I do find it in Jesus in this story.

A few years ago, someone from Scottish Churches World Exchange gave me a copy of this Charter for Visitors. It was prepared by a group of Asian hosts, preparing to welcome Scottish volunteers. Though written for that context, it seems to me to be applicable in any situation where we find ourselves in dialogue, encountering another country, another religion, another race, another reality. The words in brackets are mine.

- Travel in a spirit of humility, and with a genuine desire to learn more about the people of your host country. Be sensitively aware of the feelings of other people, thus preventing what might be offensive behaviour on your part. This applies very much to photography (or, snap judgements).

- Cultivate the habit of listening and observing, rather than simply hearing and seeing.

- Realise that people in the country you visit have different ways of thinking, and different ideas about time. This does not make them inferior, only different.

- Instead of looking for that 'beach paradise' (or what you want to be there) discover the enrichment of seeing a different way of life, through new eyes.

- Acquaint yourself with local customs. What is courteous in one country may be offensive in another. People will be happy to help you.

- Instead of the Western habit of pretending to know all the answers, cultivate the habit of asking questions.

- Remember that you are only one among what may be thousands of visitors or tourists, and do not expect special privileges.

- When you are shopping, remember that the bargains you obtain may be possible only because of the low wages paid to the maker. (Or, if you want to get something, remember that you may get it only because you hold the greater power in the encounter.)

- Do not make promises to people in your host country unless you can carry them through.

- Spend time reflecting on your daily experience in an attempt to deepen your understanding. Try to ensure that what enriches you does not degrade others.

Different maps for the same ground

Hard enough as it is to affirm that people are different, and will remain different when we are neighbours with adjoining territories, it is nothing to the difficulty of having different maps for the same piece of ground. There is a particular intensity, a particular ferocity even, about the internal conflict, the divided country, the civil war. Which map shall be the dominant one? Will it be the Unionist map or the Nationalist map for Northern Ireland, the Zionist map or the Palestinian map for the West Bank and East Jerusalem, the Serbian map or the Albanian map for Kosovo? Will it be the economic growth map or the green map? What will the family map look like, the childhood one, the religious one? Should the map in a violent society include the right to carry guns or their banning? Should the map of being a women include the choice to have an abortion or its prohibition? The internal conflicts within individuals can maim and damage for life – which part of our divided self will win? And who will decide, and how?

For a faith whose founder was unequivocal in teaching that his followers should love their enemies, do good to those who hate them, bless those who curse them and pray for those who ill-treat them, and who died doing exactly that, Christians have been remarkably willing to embrace war and engage in conflict. They have been, and are, found on both sides of every conflict, and have often been prepared to kill, not only to defend their own side but aggressively to obliterate the other side. Far fewer have been mediators, negotiators or conflict resolvers.

It is hard sometimes to understand why the resolution of conflict should have received such low priority in the history of the Christian church, for even where mediation has gone on, sometimes pursued with great patience and at great cost, it is overlooked, downplayed and often all but invisible.

It is not, of course, suprising to find Christians showing up on different sides. The unavoidable fact of difference, of being en-culturated into time, place, culture, tribal identity and all the other components of being human make it inevitable. The self-interest of the group or individual, and the drive to conformity within that, is a powerful force and we are full of human frailty. And besides, for millions of poor or subject peoples, the fighting of wars was never a matter of choice but of coercion.

Nor is it surprising to find Christians passionate in the cause of justice, and against oppression, slavery, profound and preventable human suffering. One cannot stand in the line of Isaiah, Amos, Micah, Jesus, however small and shaky one is in that line, without a burning sense of anger and urge to right glaring wrongs. For as many people who fought in the Second World War out of motives of fear, greed, hatred and racism, there must have been as many who fought reluctantly but committedly out of the desire to halt a very fearful evil.

Nevertheless, in all the border conflicts, civil wars and open warfare on a global scale, the responses of the Christian church have mirrored those outside it, and indeed, have so often been the originator, that when the image of Christ shines out, in a Franz Jagerstatter or a Martin Luther King, it makes the contrast all the more stark.

The prevalent human responses to conflict show up as much in the religious stance as in the secular. The biologically programmed *'fight'* response sees the conflict as a win–lose situation, us or them. It is prepared to embitter relationships in the process in order to win. Because it comes from the perception of being threatened, and sees the conflict as a survival issue, it will go to any lengths to be in control, and will avoid showing feelings of fear and weakness. In order to attempt to bring a Christian perspective of checks and balances to bear in such a situation, and to try to draw guidelines for military engagement, the 'just war' theory was developed from the Middle Ages onwards. For many since then, the principles of the 'just war' have been a standard to be followed with much conscientious and agonized decision-making. For others, it has simply been a convenient justification for doing what they wanted in order to get what they wanted.

The *'flight'* response has been to stay away from the conflict as much as possible, to distance itself, ignore or avoid it, hope it will go away. Conflict avoidance is usually born of feelings of powerlessness or hopelessness about the outcome, of fear that the costs will be too high, that resources are too limited and therefore that action is useless. The church has done a lot of this too, withdrawing into quietism and pietism, detaching itself from the world, sometimes taking advantage of a privileged status to avoid conflict.

And of course, there is always a lot of *compromise*, of trying to find the best solution in the circumstances, of appeasing, looking for the middle ground. We all do it, and the church does it quite well. But still, there is such a longing among so many ordinary people for an approach to conflict that goes deeper. We are so aware of the cost of war – we have, after all, lived in the twentieth century, the century of the Somme and Auschwitz, of Hiroshima and Stalin and the gulags, of the killing fields of Cambodia and Rwanda. We are so aware of the failure of war to solve things, only to shift the balance of power a little, of revolutions that replaced one set of injustices with another.

But we are also aware of the repression, the torture, the inequalities, the slavery, the cruelty, the grinding poverty, the exclusion and sense of being utterly expendable that makes people rise up and say, 'enough is enough'. We do not want to sit back and do nothing, we are not comfortable about retreating into pietism, even if it is dressed up in the modern garb of exploring our own spirituality.

Even our compromises look shabby and complicit. They leave basic issues unresolved, covered up, waiting to surface again when the stakes are raised. These things always happened – but now they happen nightly on our television screens, and we can no more plead ignorance.

> the crunch of things breaking
> the earth heaving up entrails
> blood dripping into the ground
> a child sobbing
>
> the zen of war
> (to be most lethally accurate
> aim wide of the target)
>
> the correspondents duck
> in the lobby
> the Red Cross waits
> > (KG, 'open warfare', 1997)

What does it mean, to work for conflict resolution, for *problem-solving*? What does it mean to try to look for the real issues, concerns and fears in the situation, to recognize that the problem is a shared responsibility? What does it mean to try to understand and address the needs and grievances of everyone concerned, to acknowledge the issues of injustice which are present? What does it mean to proceed by these principles of non-violence, commitment to a 'just peace'?

- respect for the opponent as a fellow human being
- care for everyone involved in a conflict
- refusal to harm, damage or degrade people/living things/the earth

121

- if suffering is inevitable, the readiness to take it upon oneself rather than inflict it on others
- not retaliating to violence with violence
- belief that everyone is capable of change
- appeal to the humanity of the opponent
- recognition that no one has a monopoly of truth, so trying to bring together different truths
- belief that the means are the ends in the making, so the means have to be consistent with the ends
- openness rather than secrecy

For sure, it means work, patience, sensitivity, sacrifice far beyond what we are accustomed to expect or give, even in the church. And it means being prepared to suspend cynicism and live out of hope, the belief that what we do will make a difference, will not be lost. For of course these principles are not shared by Saddam Hussein and of course the British government is not going to adopt them as its defence policy, nor any other government that I can think of. But because we cannot adopt them at the macro-level should not stop us adopting them at the micro-level. There are so many local conflicts, so many miniature wars, so many divided groups and individuals where the other answers are just not working.

Women will not readily go back to a time when they would endure regular beatings from their partners at the injunction of the church. They have recognized that to do so is not only to accept a devalued status as human for themselves, but is to be complicit in another person's injustice. They will separate, remove themselves from another's overwhelming need to be dominant. But this does not mean their wish is to see abusers in their turn be degraded, dehumanized and controlled. We have children, female and male, and we love them all. We want there to be instead a culture which does not glorify violence, which does not represent it a thousand ways every day in our media as an ideal of strength and power. If we start small, where we can, in mediation, in negotiation, in conflict resolution, if we pay attention to the boundary disputes before they grow into internecine warfare, perhaps we can begin to create a culture of right relationship rather than a culture of violence, a world in which it is so easy to go to war.

And if even a tenth of the money that is spent worldwide on armaments was diverted into training, resourcing and encouraging the skills of peacemaking, mediation and conflict resolution, perhaps we might live in a safer world. It would be a good investment in the future.

CROSS-BORDER PEACE TALKS

There is a place
beyond the borders
where love grows,
and where peace is not the frozen silence
drifting across no man's land from two heavily defended
entrenchments,
but the stumbling, stammering attempts of long-closed throats
to find words to bridge the distance;
neither is it a simple formula
that reduces everything to labels,
but an intricate and complex web of feeling and relationship
which spans a wider range than you'd ever thought possible.

That place is not to be found on the map
of government discussions
or political posturing.
It does not exist within the borders of
Catholic or Protestant,
Irish or British,
male or female,
old or young.
It lies beyond,
and is drawn with different points of reference.

To get to that place,
you have to go
(or be pushed out)
beyond the borders,
to where it is lonely, fearful, threatening,
unknown.
Only after you have wandered for a long time
in the dark,
do you begin to bump into others,
also branded,
exiled,
border-crossers,
and find you walk on common ground.

It is not an easy place to be,

this place beyond the borders.
It is where you learn that there is more pain in love than in hate,
more courage in forbearance than in vengeance,
more remembering needed in forgetting,
and always new borders to cross.

But it is a good place to be.

(KG, 1995)

8

The Story
So Far ...

A few years ago, I took part in the making of a number of
television programmes for BBC Scotland whose series title
was *The Story So Far*. It was about different kinds of stories: there
were stories of people, from the Gospels and from the lives of Celtic
Christians many centuries ago and of a number of women and men
living in the same places today, because these were also stories of
place, of remote and rocky corners of Scotland, Ireland, Wales,
Cornwall, Brittany. For a couple of months I travelled with an
eclectic collection of saints with names like Ninian and Brigid,
Ichtyd and Mochoi, Columba and Kevin. And not only saints, there
were angels too, 'archs' and guardians, Gabriel and Raphael and
most of all Michael, *cra-gheal*, Michael the red-white, chieftain of
the needy, bright warrior, the one who meets the soul and leads it
home. You cannot travel in these western fringes of Europe and
encounter saints and angels without getting caught up in their story.
For these few weeks, I fell under their spell, lived within the myth,
the poetry, the vision.

But as I was travelling with a television crew and production
team, I came to realize that we ourselves, with all our twentieth-
century stories, were also becoming part of the same story, that as
we encountered this history, these people, we were ourselves
becoming the next chapter in 'the story so far ...'

The connection between the world
that pushed men to the Atlantic fringes
to make a heart out of a quiet cell
and this one where we arrive in cars,
wrestle through the night to make things work
and grumble over breakfast

is not immediately apparent.
But it's there.
In part it is the ground we stand on,
the same rock, tree, water.
But mostly, it's the story;
story seen, story heard, story lived.
The difference is mainly in the technology.
The connection is the story.
And this story is the harvest of that story.

(KG)

Over many years as a member of the Iona Community (including several spent living on Iona itself), as the editor of the Community's magazine, and as someone who engages in some theological and liturgical reflection in its name, the phenomenon that is the renaissance of interest in all things Celtic has become very familiar to me. And, as my television experience taught me, I have not myself been immune to it. Over the last ten years, books, programmes, conferences and pilgrimages have welled up in a trickle that has become a flood.

And though members of the Iona Community can sometimes be overheard muttering darkly, or sighing mournfully, according to temperament, when the words 'Celtic spirituality' are mentioned, deep down we know how significant a renaissance it is. It is, in effect, a rediscovery of a 'history not part of history'. There are many strands of the richly coloured tapestry that is Christianity which have been overlooked, hidden under the dust of ages, or even deliberately neglected because their patterns did not accord with the prevailing fashion or the dominant world-view.

We have many questions about those who went before us in these islands, who evangelized our ancestors in the faith, and whose spirituality, tenacious for centuries, was eventually superseded by those which looked to Rome and to Canterbury and to Geneva, and which spoke in different mother tongues. Some of our questions are being answered now, with a degree of accuracy, by historians and archaeologists, by theologians and human ecologists. Others are subject to conjecture, poetic imagination and the wilder flights of romantic Celtic fantasy in which there is nothing more important than a good story. Many questions remain forever unanswerable, on the other side of the chasm of time.

Speaking for myself, though I have been much enlightened and enriched by what I have learned of Celtic culture, I have come to be less interested in the answers and more interested in the questions – or at least, the questioners. On Iona, in the Iona Community, and in many conversations that have been evoked by as little as people's discovery that I am a Scot, there has been an eagerness that I would not hesitate to describe as amounting to a hunger to know more of these people and their faith. Interestingly, this hunger I have found most evident among people who are *not* Scots or Irish or Welsh, though it is there also. What yearning, what need of the heart and spirit is being expressed here? This is more than just historical interest. There is a sense in it of people seeking to bring all their exiles home – not just exiled parts of their history but, through that, the exiled parts of their lives.

Every day, as people of faith, we struggle to select the features of real significance, to discern the meaning of, and meaning in our lives. But for many people, and perhaps even sometimes for us, the doctrines and practices of the church mask or exclude some features of real significance. Signs and symbols have become disordered: bread and wine more evocative of division than communion; servanthood and authority hopelessly confused; the incarnation, the Word made flesh, somehow tied up in people's minds with a rejection of the body.

If one asks the enquirer into Celtic spirituality, as I often do, what appeals to them about it, the answers are fairly uniform: the sense of God present in the creation, in nature; the sense of God present in the everyday, in the ordinary things of life, delight in creativity, in art, in the love of story and song; a love of pilgrimage and of wandering; missionary zeal which nevertheless did not impose alien systems but adapted existing traditions; a sense of community. Those whose grasp on fact is somewhat hazier also often refer to more egalitarian forms of leadership and an enhanced status for women. You would be harder pressed to find these, but never mind – they, along with the other things, are what are being looked for!

And Celtic spirituality shares a significant feature with feminist, indigenous and mystical spiritualities: the affirmation of the feeling, the affective and intuitive and subjective. It is not hard to see that a Christian church which is perceived to be primarily institutional and intellectual, concerned with the spiritual to the exclusion of the material, and which is, perhaps worst of all, shackled to its relentless respectability and ineffable dullness, creates many exiles.

Of course we can say, 'But the church isn't like that now, things have changed' – and to some extent that is true; but there is a price to be paid for being on the winning side of history as well. All these parts we left out, we needed them more than we thought.

Be that as it may, perhaps there is something in the soul of late twentieth-century Westerners, tied as we are to mortgages and clock-watching, to Sunday morning 11 a.m. and the routines of suburban life, that is moved by wandering, free-spirited Celts, by the resonance of rock and sand and turbulent seas, and by a faith that seems rugged and passionate and essentially life-affirming. Celtic spirituality is often referred to as integrated or holistic, as holding to the 'unitary vision' in which many paradoxes were encompassed, and indeed this notion of encompassing, of encircling, reiterated in the circular and spiral patterns of Celtic art, points to an older and less linear, less goal-directed tradition.

But it is important, I believe, for those who seek in Celtic spirituality resources for contemporary Christian faith to re-emphasize the crucial fact that for the Celts, both in the gospel and in their culture, integrity, wholeness, was not just that of the individual person. The wholeness was that of the whole community, including the community of the earth, the integrity not just that of the body personal but of the body politic. If we do not hold fast to that fact, then there is a danger of Celtic spirituality being seen simply as a path to individual, personal growth, a kind of alternative, quasi-Christian therapy. For Columba (the Celt about whom I know most), autocratic as he was, there was no such thing as the 'single person', just as there was not for Jesus. There were only persons in community, or persons who, for some reason or other, were excluded from community. The strong links of the Celtic church with Eastern Orthodoxy are echoed in the passionate attachment to the Trinity, the community of God.

Part of the hunger for the new which is driving us back to these older patterns is, I think, a pervasive sense of the failure and fragmentation of the existing ones. In 1997, the year of the fourteen hundredth anniversary of his death, on St Columba's Day I made a pilgrimage, as many people in Britain did – only mine was round the city centre of Glasgow in the company of some other members of the Iona Community. It was an appropriate thing to do: the Iona Community, after all, had its genesis not on Iona but among the shipyards and poverty of Glasgow in the Depression. Glasgow was a great mercantile city, and part of our route took us through the regenerated Merchant City, a place now of designer shops, classy cafe-bars and elegant residences. It is quite seductive to sit beside a fountain in the Italian Centre in the sun, drinking cappucino. I enjoyed it a lot! But the real cost of the coffee becomes more evident as one moves eastwards – in the unlet spaces in the Candleriggs covered market; in the tatty second-hand goods laid out on the ground at Paddy's Market; and most of all south of the river in the blasted landscape round Gorbals Church, where our pilgrimage finished. And the base of that downward spiral would become most apparent in those landless *campesinos* in Latin America whose food-growing land has been turned over to coffee production.

The image of *the market* is an attractive one when it is of traders and patter and stalls heaped high with vegetables; the reality is that the unitary vision has somehow mutated into the globalization of markets (and global recolonization can be effected now as well through economics as it ever could through invading armies); debt that crucifies countries; the international monetary system behaving worse than the worst loan sharks in Glasgow or Manchester; Japanese schoolgirls (and who knows, perhaps Scottish ones too) trading their bodies for spending money; pornographic videos being filmed in the sheds behind Paddy's Market – and there's an unerotic concept for you! Truly, in the overheard words of one woman, 'The markets are no' what they used to be.' This ideology, and this spirituality (for a spirituality is what it has become) of extrinsic worth, in which value is set by market forces, is a poison eating away at the body politic. This is no way for people who care about others to live!

We feel powerless before the market and its commodification of the public space; so we try to reclaim a little of it as sacred space. We are enticed off public transport, and we go on pilgrimage to travel with our fellows. We have almost lost the art of communal enjoyment and participation; so we retreat to private worlds, to *the household*. But even this sanctuary is not safe for so many people. For them, home is where the hurt is. Sometimes it seems quite extraordinary to me that with all the achievements of the human race, we are standing on the brink of the twenty-first century as infants in the art of peaceful negotiation, still thirled to destructive patterns of domination and control, still unable to assume responsibility for our own unmet needs, still seeking to bend others to our will. Extraordinary until I find myself doing it about twice a day. The roots of the culture of violence are embedded deeply in our society – but hey, that's private, and mostly it is easier not to look beyond the doors of the household – even the household of faith.

The single most important characteristic of the Columban church was that it was monastic. Furthermore, its monasticism, springing as it did from that of the Desert Fathers of Egypt, was ascetic in the extreme. Penitential, rigorous, attached to martyrdom, living a way of life that would terrify us with its harshness – is this what the seekers are after? A way back to the desert? A hermit's cell? Perhaps not – and yet it is where we are being led.

We hunger to bring our exiles home; we feel instinctively that we are weakened by their exclusion. We follow them like birds on the wing, that delight in nature, that creativity, that sense of heaven in ordinary. We seek homecoming – but the birds lead us instead to the cell of the hermit and the ship of the exile.

> In the deserts of the heart
> Let the healing fountain start,
> In the prison of his days,
> Teach the free man how to praise.
> (W. H. Auden, 'In memory of W. B. Yeats', 1940)

After all, they were not so different from others, these Celtic Christians: their freedom did not come apart from the cross. We see the glory, less often the grey, because it is just like our grey. But the solitude of the hermit and the heartbreak of the exile, the exhaustion of the ministry of hospitality and the back-breaking grind of physical survival, the discipline of prayer and the sheer provisionality of existence, these were where the monks of Columba embraced self-abandonment and struggled to bend their will to God's will. The poems and prayers, the creativity, the community, the extraordinary witness were the fruits of that embrace and that struggle. They came home to their freedom through their exile. And described *the cell* as their 'place of resurrection'.

I often think of these men. I think about their mothers a lot as well, because every single one of them had a mother. I wonder about their mothers' lives – were they narrow, were they constrained? And did they offer praise? What was their story? The Iona Community has a lesser known, much more ascetic centre on the Ross of Mull, and when I go there, I wonder about the quarrymen and fishermen and their mothers – and I think about the crofters cleared off their lands by good Christians and sent into another kind of exile. Did they offer praise? Reports suggest they did.

As I was coming out of St Andrew's Cathedral in Glasgow one day, a man stopped me. 'Hey, missus,' he said 'can ordinary people go into the pineapple?' (It does look somewhat like at least the top of a pineapple!) It was funny, but I found it a bit depressing. Why should ordinary people not? George MacLeod started the Iona Community because he discovered that the ordinary people of the dock area of Govan in the 1930s felt that church was 'not for the likes of us' because they were not 'respectable', not good, comfortable, middle-class citizens with well-ordered lives.

They were exiles from a faith whose founder upset respectable people to the extent that he became impossible to live with, whose friends and associates had messy, dysfunctional lives, and whose own lifestyle somewhat resembled that of a New Age traveller. And yet, the irony is that it was precisely this unremarkable, unprepared and unlikely group of friends and associates – a bunch of fishermen, ex-tax-collectors, outsiders, women – none of them priests, none of them theologically trained, none of them with much power or influence to speak of, who *were* the church in the beginning. George MacLeod told a good story about them:

There is a very old legend, and all legends that persist speak truth, concerning the return of the Lord Jesus Christ to heaven after His Ascension.

It is said that the angel Gabriel met Him at the gates of the city.

'Lord, this is a great salvation that Thou hast wrought,' said the angel. But the Lord Jesus only said, Yes.

'What plans hast Thou made for carrying on the work? How are all men to know what Thou hast done?' asked Gabriel.

'I left Peter and James and John and Martha and Mary to tell their friends, and their friends to tell their friends, till all the world should know.'

'But, Lord Jesus,' said Gabriel, 'suppose Peter is too busy with his nets, or Martha with her housework, or the friends they tell are too occupied, and forget to tell their friends – what then?'

The Lord Jesus did not answer at once; then He said in His quiet, wonderful voice: 'I have not made any other plans. I am counting on them.'

(*Govan Calling*, 1934)

The partnership of equals: not servants but friends

Part of the redrawing the maps which many churches, my own included, have been engaged in of recent years has been recognizing that old outlines of patriarchy and patronage could no longer be considered appropriate in a post-imperial, democratic society. This has involved slowly and painfully moving from patterns of leader and led, master and servant, helper and helped, strong and weak, to patterns of partnership, to relationships of greater equality, inter-dependence and reciprocity, to patterns of friendship rather than institutionalized stratification. Between women and men, young and old, clergy and laity, amongst churches, and, not least, between rich and poor. This is, in part at least, a recognition of the need of the church to affirm and include in every aspect of its decision-making those same ordinary people whose faith, courage, witness and service, unsung, often overlooked, at the time even disparaged, have been the highest expression of, and the most profoundly significant force in Christian discipleship.

But trust and partnership involve a balancing of power. Whatever the context, where one partner is seen as having the power to punish, dismiss or to enforce their wishes regardless of the wishes of the other, partnership is then heavily dependent on the goodwill of the dominant partner, and anger, fear and unwilling compliance may begin to creep into the feelings and actions of the less powerful partner. But equalizing power means one partner relinquishing power, and, even if the potential gains in trust and sharing are great, letting go of power, privilege and advantage is never easy. How rarely it happens voluntarily.

Michael Taylor, former director of Christian Aid wrote: 'Of the many reasons why partnerships do not work – lack of time to foster them, practical pressures, differences of culture and approach – one remains fundamental: the fact that the partners remain "asymmetrical" (unequal) [...] Realism suggests that equal partnerships will remain a dream for as long as unequal access to the earth's resources remain a fact' (*Not Angels but Agencies*, 1995).

Equal access is a prerequisite for equal partnerships; the spiritual task is also therefore a political task, because it means equal access to many kinds of resources, to knowledge and information, to safety, to participation in decision- and policy-making, in liturgy and theology. And it is also a balancing act, since the tensions and contradictions of power are not only vertical – between those who have much and those who have little – but also horizontal, as we are pulled this way and that between the needs and demands of the individual and the community, between the prophetic demand for justice and repentance and the pastoral need for compassion, between the necessity for mature sacrifice for the sake of the future and the equal necessity for us all, adults included, to be able to retain the child's spontaneous capacity for delight in the present moment.

The churches are engaged, to different degrees, in different ways and within the context of their different traditions, in grappling with these paradoxes – always have been, in fact; much of Paul's correspondence to his young churches deals with precisely these issues. Critique, or self-critique devoid of care and compassion becomes hard and self-righteous, and leaves people paralysed by shame, fear or hostility. But without the courage and honesty to subject ourselves to genuine self-examination, and to make necessary change, it is too easy for the abuse of power – physical, economic, political, spiritual, pastoral – to take root and spread under cover of silence or cheap grace.

True partnership, of whatever nature, always needs to move beyond these rather rigid categories to a greater understanding of shared belonging, exchange and responsibility. Perhaps a creative model of partnership for a democratic age is that of friendship –it is certainly one of the most vivid in the gospel story. The fifteenth chapter of John's Gospel offers a beautiful image of the community of faith as branches of the living vine, and true friendship as the motif for the followers of Jesus – attentive, loving, mutually respectful. It is characterized by openness and transparency (no withholding of knowledge here) and the sharing of power.

Two aspects of this image are particularly striking for me. First, it describes the Christian community as one of interrelationship, shared well-being and 'indwelling'. This mutual dependence is conveyed by the use of the verb 'remain' or 'abide' which occurs no less than ten times in the first eleven verses. The words suggest constancy of presence. It describes Jesus' relationship with God, Jesus' relationship to the community and the community's relationship to Jesus. In their belonging together, Jesus and the God who is the source of his power anticipate the possibilities of life for the community. And for the community, it describes the people who go on showing up together, hanging in with each other, just being there; far from perfect, not with all the answers, often not even quite sure why they are there at all except that somehow they know they need each other.

Individuals in the community, in this image, will prosper only in so far as they recognize themselves as part of a living, organic whole, whose fruitfulness depends on their remaining united with the vine. The image assumes connectedness and mutual accountability.

And, second, it provides a radical and fruitful image of power in the community. To look at a vine is to see that no branch has pride of place, that the branches weave in and out of one another, making it impossible to tell where one stops and another begins. All are rooted in the vine, and only bear fruit as a result of their common root. I find the story of God the gardener, pruning and training the vine so that it will bear good fruit, is one which moves me to the depth of my soul. Since God is the gardener, all the branches are equal before God, and the future of the vine is entrusted to God, not to any of the branches. In it, one cannot prioritize by gender or race or sexuality or status or virtue. Only the central vine, the one from which all others grow, is clearly identifiable.

But it is not just the beauty and energy of the vision of community and mutuality that moves me. It is that it gives me a way to relate creatively to the difficult and painful struggles of my life. We all have experience of the dead branches of our lives being broken off – the relationships which have become utterly sterile, the cherished dreams dashed, the beliefs that no longer sustain us, that we see now to have been false, the old habits and ways of thinking that trip us up at every turn. We know they are dead wood, we feel their weight, feel them draining life out of us and out of others, but we also know how bitter a process it is to cut them off, how much it will hurt, what new demands it will make of us to be without them. We are not sure we want to be whole, want to be healed, if this is what it will take. And then life, both ruthless and merciful, comes along and does it for us anyway! It helps me to visualize this as a necessary pruning process, to see it as not only hurting but also hopeful. And because it is so bruising, it is vital for me to remember that it takes place in the context of connectedness, of being part of the vine. It is a properly therapeutic process, and quite a good description of what goes on all the time in pastoral and counselling and therapeutic relationships.

It matters so much to so many people that we find new relationships to power and power-sharing, because we live in a world where so many are damaged by distorted relationships and power imbalances. Perceptions of the Christian church are often that it participates in this imbalance. Either it is seen as seeking and embracing power of many kinds, as a kind of extension, a worldly wielding, of the power owed to a triumphant and all powerful god-king; or it is seen as advocating a kind of passive, martyred, doormat powerlessness. Or, worst of both worlds, the triumphalist wielders of power are seen as urging that on the already disem-powered, while holding on for grim death to their own power.

Of course these are caricatures, stereotypes; and yet their persistence owes much to the bad practices, concealment and lack of integrity which blighted the childhoods of many who, thankfully, fought back against being frightened or bullied into religion. It is perhaps by the grace of God that so many still are able to see beyond the terrible things done in his name to a Jesus who seemed to do things in a different way. For the stories of Jesus are, over and over again, of a man quite clearly empowered in himself, possessed of an interior authority not dependent on external authorization, but one who freely shared power with others, gave it away so that they could have more. More power, not *over* but *to*: to realize their potential, to restore their community, to stand up, to be whole, undivided people once again. In a developmental context it would be described as 'capacity-building'. In making sense of the meaning of the divinity of Jesus, I find it helpful to think of him as a totally empowered person who gave of that power freely, ultimately emptying himself of it in order to liberate it into a whole com-munity.

I once met a Scots woman who had struggled for years with alcoholism and an abusive relationship. But she said, 'My church couldn't help me because they got me stuck in the powerlessness of the crucifixion. It was only when I discovered the power of the resurrection that I found the hope to break free.' She stopped drinking, refused absolutely to tolerate any more abuse (and, though it took many years of separation, ultimately restored the relationship), and found a new worth and vocation in her life.

The power of Jesus, and, we are told, the power of the Holy Spirit given at Pentecost, was given freely in order to be shared, to build up the whole community – rather like bread, in fact. It is not too fanciful to imagine power in the same way, needing to be broken to be shared, to be poured out like wine. This nourishment, this great resource of Christianity, like a well we draw on, is drained of its meaning if it is not shared. The sacrament of communion would be unthinkable if the bread was not broken and shared. The same ought to be true of the power of the Spirit, the power *to*! Because to share the Spirit, as to share the bread, is above all to participate in *hope*, to be a community of hope, to be people who refuse to accept exclusion and violence and worthlessness as the final word, to be people who bear witness that goodness is stronger than evil, love is stronger than hate and life is stronger than death. We cannot bear witness to this hope if in practice we seek power over, refuse to share power, or enjoin the acceptance of powerlessness upon others.

Bearing witness to hope is also a question of language. As followers of Jesus, we struggle with what it means to articulate that story and experience and vision with those who do not speak the (often incomprehensible) language of the church. Yet we are called to give testimony. There is a beautiful phrase in Robert Browning's poem, *The Ring and the Book*. He says, 'testimony stoops to mother tongue', and I immediately have an irrepressible picture of a mother getting down on the floor beside her small child, coming alongside to use that lovely language of communication that is not just words but sound, and not just sounds but attentiveness, listening, encouragement. Mother tongue is the language of the heart. The church overuses the language of the head, discursive, propositional. It has, of course, a valued place – but not in testimony. It does not move us; it is too often critical, judgemental, condemnatory even. Heart needs to speak to heart.

That was the extraordinary gift of Pentecost – each one hearing the good news in her or his own mother tongue. We need to be always returning to our mother tongue, to that place where God our mother speaks to us in the language of love, nurturing, encouraging, drawing us out, setting us on our feet and pointing us in new directions. And we need to be sensitive to what is the mother tongue of others – listening, learning to hear and understand it, even to speak it. We cannot always expect others to learn our language if we want to share testimony.

But the language of faith is not just about the movement of the heart. Language is also a powerful tool. It describes and symbolizes and shapes our images and perceptions of God, of people, of the world. It encodes understandings of power. The language we use in worship, preaching, theology, testimony, does not describe the nature of God, who cannot be contained within the confines of human language (though it may describe attributes of God), but above all describes the nature of our relationship with God.

And historically, the relationship of people with God has been described in ways that emphasize to an extreme degree the experience of the *transcendence* of God. These include such titles as Almighty, Immortal, Invisible, Ineffable, Godhead, Beginning and Ending, Omnipotent and many others. The relationship has also been conditioned by the social and political structures of human power, and has emphasised the *power* of God in such terms. We are saturated with titles and images such as King, Sovereign, Monarch, Judge, Most High. Some of our images derive from the idea of the royal court. This is not necessarily a positive image today, and may be confusing. Today, a court is much more likely to suggest a court of law (or even something else).

. . . AND IS SEATED AT THE RIGHT HAND OF GOD

Where's that?
Right from what angle?
Why sitting?

The language of the royal court.
But the royal court is, to me, a theatre.
So perhaps, an actor turned director,
interpreter of story,
lover of the play,
close to the author's mind,
encourager of many outcomes,
improvisings
explorations,
yet always attentive to the inner structure, rhythm;
stretching forms,
allowing creativity,
respectful of the actors, and,
though clear about their shortcomings,
responsive to requests for help.

Yes.
This has meaning for me.
This I can trust.

(KG, 1996)

This emphasis is heightened when it is translated into images of the *might* of God. Battleshield, Defender, Deliverer, Captain, Sword for the Fight, and that great favourite, Lord of Hosts (God of Armies): our language for worship abounds with military metaphors.

And the relationship has been conditioned and shaped by a view of familial relationships which is hierarchical, vertical and masculine – Father, Son, Holy Ghost. No daughters, sisters, grandmothers or aunts – but also no cousins, uncles, grandfathers, nephews, at least in Western devotional language. All of us, male and female alike, may be acceptably described as sons of God and brothers of one another, or as children. All other relational titles are still considered to be at best unorthodox and at worst unacceptable. The only exception to this male dominance is the model above all it is impossible to aspire to – that of the virgin mother. The family language for God emphasizes the *patriarchy* of God.

Some of these titles and images may hold great meaning for people. Their significance may not be related to their actual meaning, but more to their familiarity or their metaphorical impact in certain situations. If you ask people what they actually believe when they are singing 'Lord of Hosts', not all that many actually are comfortable with a God of Armies. Nevertheless, this language shapes at a deep level the nature of our relationship with God, and may make it one which does not represent the culture in which people are attempting to live out that relationship.

To create more mature and balanced partnerships, we need to find language and images for bearing witness in worship and theology and work which allow us to relate in a fuller way to God, so that we may name our experience of the *immanence* of God, God-with-us, as well as the transcendence of God, of the vulnerability and weakness of God as well as the power and might of God. And a language of the family that suggests intimacy, mutuality and a wider vision of being family (such as pertains in the extended families of much of the world, and is beginning to show up in their language for worship as it shakes itself loose from the Western-imposed conventions), rather than the property and posterity model that is the bottom line of patriarchy.

This will require us to be creative, observant, open and imaginative. Vulnerability and weakness, intimacy and mutuality, God-with-us, are seen in places and among people who are very often ignored by the language of the church, except as objects of piety and patronage – the very poorest people, children, the frail and old, rough sleepers and people with AIDS, beaten and wounded armies, those who are excluded, messy families and so on. But we do not look among them for our models of God – which is curious, really, because that is exactly what Jesus did!

Language reflects the dominant patterns of a culture. But it is also used to reinforce them. That is why totalitarian states silence the artists and poets and journalists first – and why capitalist ones buy them – to avoid the patterns of power being subverted. The current trend of mocking 'political correctness' is no more than a pathetic and shabby excuse for failing to do justice.

They held up a stone.
  I said, 'Stone.'
Smiling they said, 'Stone.'

They showed me a tree.
  I said, 'Tree.'
Smiling they said, 'Tree.'

They shed a man's blood.
  I said, 'Blood.'
Smiling they said, 'Paint.'

They shed a man's blood.
  I said, 'Blood.'
Smiling they said, 'Paint.'

(Dannie Abse, adapted from the Hebrew of Amir Gilboa, 1982)

If our naming of our relationship with God is left so one-sided, so distorted, then partnership becomes impossible, for we are complicit with a context in which abuse, concealment and disregard for the vulnerable can flourish. And it also makes a nonsense of our liturgy, whose meaning is 'the work of the people'. The last time I looked at the church (in fact, every time I look) I see that the people include women as well as men (and mostly in the majority), children as well as adults, black people as well as white people, poor people as well as wealthy people, people who were not brought up in the church as well as people who were, people with disability as well as able-bodied people, and so on. Surely, if it truly is the work of the people, they might also expect to have their experience, their hopes and aspirations, their failures and regrets, their gifts and insights, their words and images presented in the offering of worship. By what authority, and in whose interest are they excluded? Not God's. Not theirs. Surely not the Body of Christ, of which they are also members. Or is it the case that the church institutionally does not, in its heart of hearts, trust the excluded people, may even fear the challenge they present?

There has been much work done in the last twenty years or so in the task of naming and reclaiming. But as long as people feel they have to apologize for and justify including the language of the female, the black, the poor, the marginalized in our bearing witness, then there is still much ground-clearing to be done for partnership.

The art of testimony

I am someone whose mother tongue is the language of poetry. That is not to say that I speak in rhyming couplets; rather, it is that poetry is my heart-language, the tongue which moves me, stirs me, gets me going, in which I find the expression of my deepest motivations and intuitions, just as for others the language is that of music, of painting, of dance or sport or mathematics or philosophy. I have been immersed from an early age in the poetry of the Bible, and of the songs and ballads and literature of Scotland. More lately, the poetry of liturgy, of struggle, of feminism, of the theatre, have all deepened my love of this language. But not just as a reader and writer, but also as an editor, I have to think about, and people sometimes ask me, what makes a good poem.

And there are similarities between art and testimony. They are both about bearing witness. They are both 'sent out' (this is the derivation of the word 'mission' from the Latin, *missio* 'a sending out'), offered to any who will be open to receive them. Good art (whether it is a poem, a painting, a piece of music or a play) is first of all a subjective matter. What we know about it above anything else is that it speaks to us in some way, it communicates.

Gradually, or with all the suddenness of shock, something is revealed. We see in a new way. Or, it describes an experience which, though the details may be different, evokes in us an echo – yes, I have also experienced that, wondered that, felt that. We feel a sense of something recognized. And the best art fires our imagination sufficiently to make us want to respond, to go beyond the bounds of the art into our lives. It takes us to a new place, moves us to a different way of being.

Revelation – a new way of seeing, *recognition* – a new way of knowing what we know, *imaginative possibility* of a new way of being: all good art has the potential to offer these things. But the artist has no way of either knowing or controlling what the response of the other will be, nor should they, because that is to limit the possibility of response and to make the other less than free. Full response is only possible if it is free, not coerced. What moves the other is part of the mysterious dynamic of exchange which someone of faith might understand as the action of the Holy Spirit, and which can be described but never fully comprehended in empirical terms.

So the first thing the artist (and perhaps also the giver of testimony) has to let go of is her or his attachment to outcomes, results and ends. They must simply do the work of their art. That work is always a meeting of content (that which they wish to communicate or discover or resolve) and form, the way or means used to do that. Good art requires a number of things in order for content and form to have integrity, to be a seamless garment in which not the joins but the robe is presented. It requires:

- the passionate *engagement* of the artist with his or her subject, as something that matters to them;
- a commitment to *honesty*, to speaking one's truth as far as one knows it;
- *openness* to what may emerge, and therefore,
- willingness to take a *risk*;
- faithfulness to the process of the art, to its *journey*, knowing that after it, one will not be in the same place;
- the discipline of *choice*, deciding on this word, this stroke, this note and not another.

When people do the work of art, they are wrestling with some constraint, some problem, some limitation; the problem of how to show a field of daffodils to someone who has not seen them; of expressing a feeling or idea that is struggling to get out; of exploring their depths to find meaning, understanding. In musical terms, this is a tension looking for a resolution. The form is the tools or methods or structure at the artist's disposal – language, paint, movement, sound and so on.

And form also has its requirements. It needs:

- to be *consistent* with its content – one cannot suggest a sunny landscape with black paint (or a message of love with the language of threat);
- to use a medium which others will understand, or at least have enough point of *contact* to find a way into;

- to be *faithful to its own needs*, its own internal rhythm and pace, otherwise others will receive a mixed message and will conclude it is untrustworthy;

- to be *sensitive to the constraints of its space*, be it canvas or paper or stage, or it will lose its tension and therefore there will be no resolution.

If art is a tension looking for a resolution, it will communicate where that finds echoes in the listener, reader, viewer. The geological fault line that is the San Andreas Fault is there all the time, but it is only when people become aware of it and name it that its rumblings speak. Until that point, it is abstract, theoretical, will not speak. I think it is rather similar with the theological fault line. Testimony, like art, like prayer, flowers on the knife-edge of experience. Because it is on the knife-edge, at the limits of our experience, ability, faith, strength, that we have to imagine, create, find new life – or be beaten and die. This is our experience of the cross. But for people for whom the Jesus story speaks of their lives, this is also ultimately the place of hope. It is the place of promise that the beatenness, the failure, the despair, the death is not the end of the story, and that new life is not achieved but received, comes as grace, as resurrection.

In the end, art, and the responses to it, are a mystery, and its mystery evades us, cannot be pinned down. We can analyse it, interpret it, dissect it, but our explanations are not finally satisfactory. We know it because it comes alive for us. It lives. The vast majority of us cannot become great artists in paint or words or music or dance, though we can enjoy sharing in them. And there are other arts many of us can participate in: the art of parenting, the art of citizenship, the art of friendship. But the art of testimony, of bearing witness, is one that above all requires embodiment, to be given flesh. For it is not just something we do but something we are, with all of the complex, delicate, diverse patterns of history and geography, of culture and experience, of choice and chance that makes us uniquely who we are.

This book has been a reflection on many questions. Questions of meaning, of belonging, of identity and values, questions of care and difference. In looking at the things which have shaped my answers, however tentative, to these questions, and in listening to the stories of how other people have answered them, I see how much factors of gender, family, faith, place, politics, time and so on, shape us, and make certain responses and understandings, if not inevitable, then at least highly probable. I am irrevocably marked, and not always in ways I like, or am even aware of, by being a woman, a Scot, a Christian of the Presbyterian tradition, even simply by being born in the second half of the twentieth century. These marks will by now be quite evident to anyone who has got this far in the book. They are simply part of who I am, and it it always my hope that my particular marks will be acceptable enough to allow me my own equal small space in the world, without expecting that they should entitle me to any more than that, or at anybody else's expense.

But as well as these marks, which I share with all the others with whom I am connected by virtue of our all being human, I also bear marks which are unique and particular only to me. No one else in the long sweep of humanity has been quite the same: no one has had the same DNA, the same body, the same history, quite the same collection of personal and political experiences, the same dreams and memories. I am that baby who lay in a pram under a tree in a certain garden in South-West Scotland and gurgled at the sky. I am the woman who bore my children, who learned to love solitude, who is preoccupied with laundry, who loves the view from my front step, who fell in love with these people and not others, who made this choice and not that, who has these faults and failings and those skills and interests, whose life is not well ordered and tranquil but is a whole messy conglomeration of relationships and anxieties and unresolved issues and passionate angers and equally passionate loves, of achievements and failures and attempts to take a long view, of opinions and prejudices and enthusiams, who is driven by desire and attachment which hurt as well as heal. At every turn in the road, I might go in one direction rather than another, and I do not know how much of who I am, and why, is a question of fate, of determinism, of choice, or of vocation. This is an unanswerable question. Another might interpret my life and circumstances in a completely different way from me. But in the end, I reserve the right to interpret my own life, as I respect that right for others. No one else lives it but me.

And somehow, I showed up as someone who heard my name called, and answered in the way I did. Hearing one's name happens in different ways – in a blinding flash, as it did to Paul; tenderly, in the voice of love, to Mary; doubtfully, with many unresolved questions, to Thomas; shamedly, in the voice of forgiveness to Peter. Sometimes it happens out of great clamour, sometimes in the cadences of language, sometimes in stillness and silence and emptiness. It always strikes me vividly that in the old dispensation, Jacob had to wrestle all night with the angel to be named, and he limped away wounded. In the new dispensation, the name comes to us by grace, received not achieved. I do not even know how or where or when it happened to me, that I heard my name, only that somehow that naming has become the screen through which I understand my life.

Because I am not really a very 'churchy' person by temperament, and feel as often as not that I belong more with people outside the church than inside it, and certainly that I have more in common with those, I am always struggling to find a way of bearing witness that expresses to them what that naming means to me, and what the fact of Jesus means to me. But though I am often not at ease with the church, at least in its institutional expression, I am nevertheless profoundly grateful for all the people whose testimony made mine possible – for the Quakers who quietly make peace from the strength of their inner light and the Baptists who stand up for what they believe is right; for the Anglicans facing the conflicts others conceal and the Catholics who live on the margins. And for Presbyterians, for the priesthood of all believers. But most of all for the ordinary people who love their neighbours whom they can see in response to the God whom they cannot see. Somewhere in this experience, often hidden under a huge weight of disappointment and frustration and all the things that bury it, it is there, something precious – *a story to live by*.

> O God,
> you have made us for yourself,
> and against your longing there is no defence.
> Mark us with your love,
> and release in us a passion for your justice
> in our disfigured world;
> that we may turn from our guilt and face you,
> our heart's desire.
>
> (Janet Morley, 1992)

Sources and Acknowledgements

Unless otherwise stated, the Scriptures are quoted from the *Good News Bible* published by The Bible Societies/HarperCollins Publishers Ltd UK © American Bible Society, 1966, 1971, 1976, 1992. The text of the Authorized Version of the Bible (AV) is the property of the Crown in perpetuity.

Abse, Dannie, poem adapted from the Hebrew of Amir Gilboa, in *Way Out in the Center* (Hutchinson Publishing Group, London, 1982).

Auden, W. H., 'In Memory of W. B. Yeats' in *Collected Shorter Poems 1927–1957* (Faber & Faber, London, 1966).

'Be Thou My Vision', vv. 1 and 4, translated from the Ancient Irish by Mary Byrne (1880–1931), versified by Eleanor Hull (1860–1935), in *The Church Hymnary*, 3rd ed. (Oxford University Press, Oxford, 1973).

Burgess, Ruth, 'Coming Home', in Kathy Galloway (ed.), *Pattern of Our Days: Liturgies and Resources for Worship* (Wild Goose Publications, Glasgow, 1996).

Cramb, Erik, Extract from *Tayside Industrial Mission Annual Report*, 1990.

Galloway, Kathy, '... the resurrection of the body ...' and '... and is seated at the right hand of God ...', in *Talking to the Bones* (SPCK, London, 1996).
—'de-contamination', 'drawing the lines of engagement' and 'open warfare', from 'Peace Processes', in *Coracle* 3/34 (Iona Community, Glasgow, June 1997).

—'Cross-Border Peace Talks', in *Pushing the Boat out: New Poetry* (Wild Goose Publications, Glasgow, 1995).
—all other quotations in this book marked 'KG' are hitherto unpublished pieces.

Griffiths, Ann (d. 1805), 'I Saw Him Standing', translated by Rowan Williams, in *After Silent Centuries* (The Perpetua Press, Oxford, 1994).

Hope, Stanley, extract from an article in *Coracle* 3/38 (Iona Community, Glasgow, February 1998).

Leonard, Tom, 'Proem', in *Lines Review* No. 134 (September 1995).

MacLeod, George, *The Whole Earth Shall Cry Glory: Iona Prayers by Revd George Macleod* (Iona Community, Wild Goose Publications, Glasgow, 1985).
—*Govan Calling* (Methuen, London, 1934).

McDonagh, Sean, *To Care for the Earth: A Call to a New Theology* (Cassell Ltd, London, 1986).

McIlvanney, William, 'In Any Street', in *These Wards-Weddings and After* (Mainstream Publishing, 1984).

McMillan, Joyce, in *Scotland on Sunday* (29 August 1993).

Merton, Thomas, *The Sign of Jonas* (Sheldon Press, London, 1976).

Morley, Janet, 'O God, you have made us...', in *All Desires Known* (SPCK, London, 1992).

Pickard, Jan Sutch, 'Treading a Path', in *Pushing the Boat Out: New Poetry* (Wild Goose Publications, Glasgow 1995).

Porritt, Jonathon, source unknown.

Taylor, Michael, *Not Angels but Agencies* (SCM/WCC, London/Geneva, 1995).

Walker, Alice, 'We Alone', and 'Love Is Not Concerned', in *Horses Make a Landscape Look More Beautiful* (copyright © 1984, Alice Walker, reprinted by permission of Harcourt Brace Jovanovich, New York, 1984).

White, Kenneth, 'Extract I' and 'Extract XV' from 'A Walk along the Shore', in *Scottish Poetry 7* (University of Glasgow Press, Glasgow, 1974).

Whitman, Walt (1819–1892), 'Miracles', in *A Year of Grace* (Victor Gollancz, London, 1950).